FAST TRACK TO SUCCESS

PROJECT
MANAGEMENT

Prentice Hall
FINANCIAL TIMES

In an increasingly competitive world, we believe it's quality of thinking that gives you the edge – an idea that opens new doors, a technique that solves a problem or an insight that simply makes sense of it all. The more you know, the smarter and faster you can go.

That's why we work with the best minds in business and finance to bring cutting-edge thinking and best learning practice to a global market.

Under a range of leading imprints, including *Financial Times Prentice Hall*, we create world-class print publications and electronic products bringing our readers knowledge, skills and understanding, which can be applied whether studying or at work.

To find out more about Pearson Education publications or tell us about the books you'd like to find, you can visit us at
www.pearsoned.co.uk

PEARSON
Education

FAST TRACK TO SUCCESS

PROJECT
MANAGEMENT

PATRICK HARPER-SMITH AND SIMON DERRY

 Prentice Hall
FINANCIAL TIMES

An imprint of **Pearson Education**

Harlow, England • London • New York • Boston • San Francisco • Toronto • Sydney • Singapore • Hong Kong
Tokyo • Seoul • Taipei • New Delhi • Cape Town • Madrid • Mexico City • Amsterdam • Munich • Paris • Milan

PEARSON EDUCATION LIMITED

Edinburgh Gate
Harlow CM20 2JE
Tel: +44 (0)1279 623623
Fax: +44 (0)1279 431059
Website: www.pearsoned.co.uk

First published in Great Britain in 2009

ISBN: 978-0-273-71992-2

British Library Cataloguing-in-Publication Data
A catalogue record for this book is available from the British Library

Library of Congress Cataloging-in-Publication Data
Harper-Smith, Patrick.
  Fast track to success : project management / Patrick Harper-Smith and Simon Derry.
    p. cm.-- (Fast track series)
  Includes bibliographical references and index.
  ISBN 978-0-273-71992-2 (pbk. : alk. paper) 1. Project management. I. Derry, Simon. II. Title. III. Title: Project management
  HD69.P75H358 2009
  658.4'04--dc22
                              2009005449

The publisher is grateful for permission to reproduce the figure on page 135 from *Effective Leadership: A Self Development Manual*, Gower Publishing (Adair, J., 1983). Reproduced by permission of the author.

10 9 8 7 6 5 4 3 2
13 12 11 10 09

Series text design by Design Deluxe
Typeset in 10/15 Swis Lt by 30
Printed by Ashford Colour Press Ltd, Gosport

The publisher's policy is to use paper manufactured from sustainable forests.

CONTENTS

THE FAST TRACK WAY

Everything you need to accelerate your career

The best way to fast track your career as a manager is to fast track the contribution you and your team make to your organisation and for your team to be successful in as public a way as possible. That's what the Fast Track series is about. The Fast Track manager delivers against performance expectations, is personally highly effective and efficient, develops the full potential of their team, is recognised as a key opinion leader in the business, and ultimately progresses up the organisation ahead of their peers.

You will benefit from the books in the Fast Track series whether you are an ambitious first-time team leader or a more experienced manager who is keen to develop further over the next few years. You may be a specialist aiming to master every aspect of your chosen discipline or function, or simply be trying to broaden your awareness of other key management disciplines and skills. In either case, you will have the motivation to critically review yourself and your team using the tools and techniques presented in this book, as well as the time to stop, think and act on areas you identify for improvement.

Do you know what you need to know and do to make a real difference to your performance at work, your contribution to your company and your blossoming career? For most of us, the honest answer is 'Not really, no'. It's not surprising then that most of us never reach our full potential. The innovative Fast Track series gives you exactly what you need to speed up your progress and become a high performance manager in all the areas of the business that matter. Fast Track is not just another 'How to' series. Books on selling tell you how to win sales but not how to move from salesperson to sales manager. Project management software enables you to plan detailed tasks but doesn't improve the quality of your project management thinking and business performance. A marketing book tells you about the principles of marketing but not how to lead a team of marketers. It's not enough.

Specially designed features in the Fast Track books will help you to see what you need to know and to develop the skills you need to be successful. They give you:

→ the information required for you to shine in your chosen function or skill – particularly in the Fast Track top ten;

→ practical advice in the form of Quick Tips and answers to FAQs from people who have been there before you and succeeded;

→ state of the art best practice as explained by today's academics and industry experts in specially written Expert Voices;

→ case stories and examples of what works and, perhaps more importantly, what doesn't work;

→ comprehensive tools for accelerating the effectiveness and performance of your team;

→ a framework that helps you to develop your career as well as produce terrific results.

Fast Track is a resource of business thinking, approaches and techniques presented in a variety of ways – in short, a complete performance support environment. It enables managers to build careers from their first tentative steps into management all the way up to becoming a business director – accelerating the performance of their team and their career. When you use the Fast Track approach with your team it provides a common business language and structure, based on best business practice. You will benefit from the book whether or not others in the organisation adopt the same practices; indeed if they don't, it will give you an edge over them. Each Fast Track book blends hard practical advice from expert practitioners with insights and the latest thinking from experts from leading business schools.

The Fast Track approach will be valuable to team leaders and managers from all industry sectors and functional areas. It is for ambitious people who have already acquired some team leadership skills and have realised just how much more there is to know.

If you want to progress further you will be directed towards additional learning and development resources via an interactive Fast Track website, **www.Fast-Track-Me.com**. For many, these books therefore become the first step in a journey of continuous development. So, the Fast Track approach gives you everything you need to accelerate your career, offering you the opportunity to develop your knowledge and skills, improve your team's performance, benefit your organisation's progress towards its aims and light the fuse under your true career potential.

ABOUT THE AUTHORS

PATRICK HARPER-SMITH is one of the founding directors of Project Leaders International Ltd – a consulting organisation that works with client companies in the areas of training, consulting and supporting software. He works with clients to establish, expand and diversify their businesses through the application of strategy, project management processes and innovation strategies.

Patrick has had a varied international career within the travel, financial services and consulting industries. At US consulting firm Kepner-Tregoe, he managed and developed highly profitable operations in the South-East Asian region. He also worked for Jacques Borel, founding and developing their voucher business in Hong Kong. At American Express he was Director of Training for the whole of South-East Asia (600 offices in Asia-Pacific and the marketing of the Corporate Card in ten Asian markets).

Patrick gained an associate degree from Université de Paris and is a pro-gramme director on the Project Leaders International strategy and innovation and project leaders programmes. He is also PRINCE2 qualified.

E Patrick.HarperSmith@Project-Leaders.net

SIMON DERRY is also a director of Project Leaders International Ltd. He is a professional consultant with over 15 years' experience of working with leading organisations in a variety of industry sectors and management levels.

Following graduation from the University College of Swansea, Simon attended the Royal Military Academy at Sandhurst and then served five years as an officer with the Royal Regiment of Artillery. In 1993 he joined the NHS as directorate manager at Northwick Park Hospital NHS Trust. He then became customer service manager for Psion in 1995, the leading hand-held computing company in the world at the time, where he established the customer services, technical support and helpdesk operations.

In 1998 he joined an international management consultancy and training firm where his remit was the design, development and implementation of service improvement projects with various clients worldwide, including Dell, Sun Microsystems, Siebel, Cisco and other IT and telecoms companies. He has detailed knowledge of the incident management and problem management aspects of the ITIL framework, and is PRINCE2 accredited.

Simon also has an MBA from Henley Management College (now Heney Business School), where he focused on project management selection systems and creativity and innovation in the workplace.

E Simon.Derry@Project-Leaders.net

A WORD OF THANKS FROM THE AUTHORS

We would like to thank the following for their generous contributions to this book.

→ **Liz Gooster, Pearson.** There are many exciting new ideas in the publishing world at present, but without an enthusiastic champion, most will simply die a slow death. Liz had the confidence to commission the Fast Track series and associated web-tool on behalf of the Pearson Group at a time when other publishers were cutting back on non-core activities. She has remained committed to its success – providing direction, challenge and encouragement as and when required.

→ **Ken Langdon.** As well as being a leading author in his own right, Ken has worked with all the Fast Track authors to bring a degree of rigour and consistency to the series. As each book has developed, he has been a driving force behind the scenes, pulling the detailed content for each title together in the background – working with an equal measure of enthusiasm and patience!

→ **Mollie Dickenson.** Mollie has a background in publishing and works as a research manager at Henley Business School, and has been a supporter of the project from its inception. She has provided constant encouragement and challenge, and is, as always, an absolute delight to work with.

→ **Critical readers.** As the Fast Track series evolved, it was vital that we received constant challenge and input from other experts and from critical readers.

→ **Professor David Birchall.** David has worked to identify and source Expert Voice contributions from international academic and business experts in each Fast Track title. David is co-author of the Fast Track *Innovation* book and a leading academic author in his own right, and has spent much of the last 20 years heading up the research programme at Henley Business School – one of the world's top ten business schools.

Our expert team

Last but not least, we are grateful for the contributions made by experts from around the world in each of the Fast Track titles.

EXPERT	TOPIC	BUSINESS SCHOOL/ COMPANY
Dr Svetlana Cicmil	Managing in complexity – project management as practical wisdom (p. 14)	Bristol Business School, University of the West of England
Dr Stephen Simister	Managing risk on projects (p. 26)	Henley Business School, University of Reading
Professor Svein Arne Jessen	Contemporary project management and leadership (p. 66)	BI Norwegian School of Management, Norway
Professor David Birchall	Improvisational working within projects (p. 86)	Henley Business School, University of Reading
Professor Stephen Wearne	Is project management a problem or an opportunity? (p. 101)	Manchester Business School, University of Manchester
Professor Kam Jugdev	Building knowledge networks in project management (p. 128)	Centre for Innovative Management, Athabasca University, Canada
Professor Christophe Bredillet	P2M, the methodology that supports the construction of complex business infrastuctures (p. 151)	ESC Lille, France
Associate Professor Dirk Pieter van Donk and Dr Eamonn Molloy	Rationality and irrationality in project management (p. 167)	Faculty of Management and Organisation, University of Groningen, The Netherlands and Saïd Business School, University of Oxford

PROJECT MANAGEMENT FAST TRACK

This book offers a very practical look at the topic of project management. So, let's start by knocking on the head a misconception that is very popular with manuals, training courses and people discussing project management; namely, that process and qualifications are the be-all and end-all of project management. Believers in this misconception concentrate on getting qualifications or using certain techniques and software, usually at the expense of the real issue – that projects are there to deliver measurable benefits and value to an organisation. Project management is about flexibility in all things and not rigid adherence to a single way of doing something. This book provides a practical framework for managing projects – not a straightjacket to hinder or restrain the project manager.

A concentration on methodologies can make us fail to relate the project to the business, leading to a ludicrous situation in which we are ticking every box on the event/activity critical path, delivering the project on time and within budget – and having no effect or even having a negative effect on the performance of the business. This may be because the project has, for example, ceased to be relevant. This is called *doing things right*. The Fast Track managers' approach is different – they are intent on *doing the right thing*. They not only relate the project objectives to the needs of the business as their starting point, but they also check that those needs have not changed during the course of running the project. The business need is paramount, not the process of getting there!

Now let's look at who classically project managers are. Project management started off in the engineering department, managing complex projects to deliver, for example, ships and aeroplanes. At that time there were full-time project managers, developing the techniques and methods that we use today. IT managers then picked up project management, realising that complex software development tasks had much in common with engineering projects. And it's moved on from there so that today many project managers are not full time; they have a day job as well, but they see project management skills as an essential tool in the Fast Track manager's armoury, no matter what their function is. Nowadays, more or less everyone is a project manager, and not necessarily running long-term projects but ones that are complete in a month, or even a week.

Take the example of sales managers charged with organising the annual sales conference. They will find that if they approach the task as a project they are much more likely to deliver a conference that is not only better than all the ones that went before, but that is also within budget and, crucially, has a positive effect on the performance of the business. This performance improvement is measurable after the conference, in terms of increased sales and profits.

We've worked, for example, with Coca-Cola marketing people: they did not regard themselves as project managers, yet when they implemented the essentials of project management to their marketing plans and promotional activities they improved performance.

So, this book is for project management professionals but it is also for non-project managers who want to use the skills of project management to improve their and their team's performance.

Although the emphasis of this book is on the practical implementation of projects to meet business needs, we do need to have some framework or structure. To that end we have developed a ten-step integrated project management process (see figure on the next page). It's been used for and with many of our clients over several years and has been updated and modified along the way. However, unlike many project management processes it is not a rigid straightjacket but a flexible approach, integrating the core best practice tools of project management with broader business needs, and involving people across the whole business, as required.

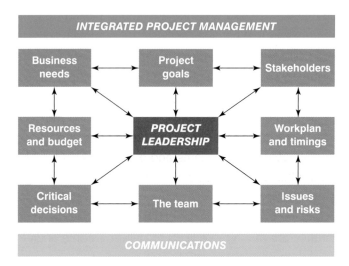

We start by assessing you and your team's current abilities in project management so that you can develop your own plan for improvement. We then show you how to link projects to business needs or identify new projects from those business needs. From there we look at the project goals and business case, checking that a successful project will deliver improved performance and achieve its measures of success.

Then you need to find out who the stakeholders are in the project, including senior management (if it is a major project), and identify anyone who could throw a spanner in the works at some point by, for example, explaining that they are undertaking a similar task. After all, if no one will sponsor the project at senior level, it's better to kill it off now than make a half-hearted go of it. Stakeholders can be both a positive and a negative influence on your project, so you need to find out who they are right at the outset and what their attitude is.

We will explain the importance of techniques such as critical path analysis, showing how to use them in the context of the business. This allows you to work out the many issues and assess the risks that you are taking in implementing the project. But implementation depends on much more than the techniques of project management; it also depends on the behaviour of the people in the project team, as well as the other stakeholders. Remember that people run projects, not software! Among other abilities, project managers need to be able to plan, to take critical decisions, to measure risk and to plan avoidance tactics. We'll help you to bring your skills up to speed. However, project management skills should be an enabler of projects rather than a set of rules to be slavishly followed. After all, the success of your business depends on the creativity and adventurousness of people – and so does every project.

Another topic is the management of resources and budgets, which are frequent sources of problems and even project failure. Notice how we've called this 'another' topic and not the final topic because in real life you will find yourself moving about these processes and employing these skills at various points in the project life cycle.

HOW TO USE THIS BOOK

Fast Track books present a collection of the latest tools, techniques and advice to help build your team and your career. Use this table to plan your route through the book.

PART	OVERVIEW
About the authors	A brief overview of the authors, their background and their contact details
A **Awareness**	*This first part gives you an opportunity to gain a quick overview of the topic and to reflect on your current effectiveness*
1 *Project management in a nutshell*	A brief overview of project management and a series of frequently asked questions to bring you up to speed quickly
2 *Project management audit*	Simple checklists to help identify strengths and weaknesses in your team and your capabilities
B **Business Fast Track**	*Part B provides tools and techniques that may form part of the integrated project management framework for you and your team*
3 *Fast Track top ten*	Ten tools and techniques used to help you implement a sustainable approach to project management based on the latest best practice
4 *Technologies*	A review of the latest information technologies used to improve effectiveness and efficiency of project management activities
5 *Implementing change*	A detailed checklist to identify gaps and to plan the changes necessary to implement your projects
C **Career Fast Track**	*Part C focuses on you, your leadership qualities and what it takes to get to the top*
6 *The first ten weeks*	Recommended activities when starting a new role in project management, together with a checklist of useful facts to know
7 *Leading the team*	Managing change, building your team and deciding your leadership style
8 *Getting to the top*	Becoming a project management professional, getting promoted and becoming a director – what does it take?
D **Director's toolkit**	*The final part provides more advanced tools and techniques based on industry best practice*
Toolkit	Advanced tools and techniques used by senior managers
Glossary	Glossary of terms

FAST-TRACK-ME.COM

Throughout this book you will be encouraged to make use of the companion site: **www.Fast-Track-Me.com**. This is a custom-designed, highly interactive online resource that addresses the needs of the busy manager by providing access to ideas and methods that will improve individual and team performance quickly. Top features include:

→ **Health Checks**. Self-audit checklists allowing evaluation of you and your team against industry criteria. You will be able to identify areas of concern and plan for their resolution using a personal 'Get-2-Green' action plan.

→ **The Knowledge Cube**. The K-Cube is a two-dimensional matrix presenting Fast Track features from all topics in a consistent and easy-to-use way – providing ideas, tools and techniques in a single place, anytime, anywhere. This is a great way to delve in and out of business topics quickly.

→ **The Online Coach**. The Online Coach is a toolkit of fully interactive business templates in MS Word format that allow Fast-Track-Me.com users to explore specific business methods (strategy, ideas, projects etc.) and learn from concepts, case examples and other resources according to your preferred learning style.

→ **Business Glossary**. The Fast Track Business Glossary provides a comprehensive list of key words associated with each title in the Fast Track series together with a plain English definition – helping you to cut through business jargon.

The website can also help answer some of the vital questions managers are asking themselves today (see figure overleaf).

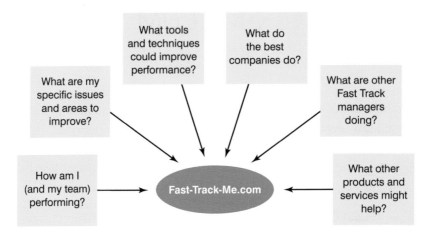

Don't get left behind: log on to **www.Fast-Track-Me.com** now to get your career on the fast track.

AWARENESS

This book introduces a sustainable approach to project management aimed at keeping you, your team and your organisation at the fore-front of the process, thus contributing towards the future of all three. The starting point is to gain a quick understanding of what project management is and what it is not, and to be aware of your own and your team's capabilities in this area right now. For this reason we will ask you a number of questions that will reveal where you and your team need to improve if you are truly to meet the aims of project management – and ensure your service to customers is among the leaders in your industry.

'Know yourself' was the motto above the doorway of the Oracle at Delphi and is a wise thought. It means that you must do an open and honest self-audit as you start on the process of setting up your frame-work for project management.

The stakes are high. Project management is at the heart of success in this global, competitive marketplace. Your team, therefore, need to be effective project managers and you need to be a good leader in project management. Poor leadership and poor team effectiveness will make fail-ure likely. An effective team poorly led will sap the team's energy and lead in the long term to failure through their leaving for a better environment or becoming less effective through lack of motivation. Leading an ineffective team well does not prevent the obvious conclusion that an ineffective team will not thrive. So, looking at the figure below, how do you make sure that you and your team are in the top right-hand box – an innovative and effec-tive team with an excellent leader? That's what this book is about, and this section shows you how to discover your and your team's starting point.

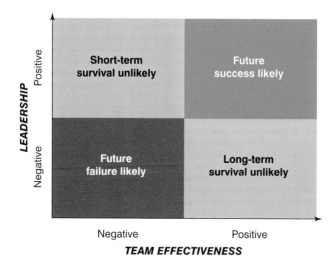

PROJECT MANAGEMENT IN A NUTSHELL

This chapter is about raising the awareness of the need for good project management techniques across an organisation. There is usually significant room for improvement in both individual and corporate capabilities, and in the effectiveness of teams in managing projects.

Starting with the basics

Just what is project management?

A quick search on the internet will reveal many varied definitions of projects and project management, but knowing many definitions doesn't make you a better project manager nor make project management any easier. Here are our definitions.

→ A **project** is a series of activities designed to achieve a specific outcome within a set budget and timescale.

→ **Project management** enables managers to focus on priorities, track performance, overcome difficulties and adapt to change. It gives managers more control and provides proven tools and techniques to help them lead teams to meet objectives on time and within budget.

Project management is not necessarily about doing the tasks included in the scope of the project, but instead it is the management or organisation of the activities included in the scope of the project. Projects are not processes and they are not routine 'business as usual'. We often forget that projects are about managing people and performance just as much as they are about planning and plans.

Why is project management so important today?

Working with our clients over the past decade or so made it clear to us that more and more managers were being 'asked' by organisations to deliver projects for their organisations. The managers in question came from a range of disciplines and professions, but almost all of them had one thing in common – none had formal project management training.

'Professional' project managers used to be found only in some large corporates who had dedicated project management offices (PMOs) involved with large strategic programmes and initiatives. In addition, many IT departments had project managers working almost continually on software development, upgrades and roll-out projects. In contrast, for the vast majority of our clients, project managers had a 'day job'. They had to fit in the management of projects along with their day-to-day line management activities. These managers were often marketing or customer service managers, who were involved from time to time in the delivery of projects for their department or the wider business.

Project management has stopped being a specialism for a few dedicated individuals and has entered the broad mainstream. We believe that it is a key management capability for the twenty-first century that all managers should acquire and develop.

This book will help you to assess your current skills and then guide you through a project management process. It will show you how to identify the activities involved in the project, how to prioritise them and how they interrelate. It will help you focus on the critical activities, estimate the risks involved and plan to avoid them or to mitigate their consequences. Finally, it will show you how to monitor your progress, anticipate problems and overcome any that occur.

This book is about acquiring and developing this management competence and deploying it not only for the business's benefit but also for your own self-development along the way. This is because project management is a skill that people will expect you to have as you rise in the business.

So why is it so difficult – what typically goes wrong?

So now we understand why project management is important, but unfortunately things still go wrong! Consider each of the following potential pitfalls and identify which, if any, will apply to you and your team, and what you can do about them quickly.

1 **The project does not have clear goals and objectives.** If project objectives are not clearly stated and understood by the project manager and their team, it is almost impossible for them to plan the relevant activities within the overall project because they simply do not know 'what to aim for'. An objective such as 'Improve customer service' does not help the team plan effective activities and does not help them assess the effectiveness of the overall project. 'Answer the phone within four rings, nine times out of ten' does.

2 **There is a lack of alignment to the business.** If projects are not aligned with the corporate strategy or to the business need, then they are in danger of helping the company improve in areas or activities that are not critical to the future direction of the organisation. If the project or its objectives are not aligned, resources are being consumed to move the company further from the goals and aspirations that the senior management team has articulated in the strategy. We have seen a project team spending time and money on a division of the business that management had already sold – good for the buyer's shareholders but not so good for shareholders of the selling company.

3 **Key sponsors and stakeholders do not play their part.** If senior sponsors do not participate in the planning, monitoring and implementation of certain projects, there are a number of negative implications for the project manager and their team: they get insufficient resources and management attention, tardy decision making delays the project and budgets may be

inadequate. If senior managers are not seen to be backing a project, functional managers and owners of resources do not see it as having a high priority. In addition, when stakeholders are not involved at the correct time, the project team may over-look important objectives or critical decisions.

4 **The team communicates its objectives poorly.** If the project has clear goals and objectives but these are not communi-cated appropriately across the team and business, then problems are going to occur during planning and implementa-tion. If they are not told, how are people expected to understand your aims and objectives?

5 **The scope of the project creeps up.** If objectives and project deliverables are not clearly established then there is a danger that the project will suffer from 'scope creep'. This means that the project will be expected to deliver more benefits than were origi-nally planned, resulting in it being late, over budget or both. If scope creep occurs then it will be even more difficult to assess the overall success of the project measured by the achievement of the project objectives. It is, however, acceptable to increase or decrease the scope of the project if that is agreed by all parties.

QUICK TIP **PLANNING**

Expect to revise your plan several times before implementation and even again when the project is underway. This is what project management is all about. Learn to accept the inevitability of change. Even with the most accurate planning, projects will change, and so the plan needs to be flexible.

---

6 **The team lacks information on their performance in the project.** If, during the planning and implementation of the project, the manager and team have no sense of what they should be doing or delivering at a given point in time, then their chances of delivering a wholly successful project are substantially reduced.

7 **People are unclear about who is responsible for what.** The simplest of mistakes often occur from a lack of basic, clear

delegation of tasks. This leads to omissions in the project – 'Oh! I thought you were doing that' – or duplication of effort, resulting in a waste of time and resources – 'We've done that, too' or 'Our part of the project covers that as well'. When time and resources are critical, there is no excuse for unclear responsibilities.

8 **The team manages and integrates external suppliers poorly.** All too often, stakeholders in a project are viewed as being only those who are internal to the project. However, external stakeholders, such as suppliers, are equally important to the successful completion of the project.

These potential pitfalls can be addressed individually, or as part of an integrated framework, such as that presented in Chapter 3. They can also be tackled as part of project or portfolio management and even be included in the monitoring of external trends and influences.

 CASE STORY *BISCUIT MANUFACTURER, SIMON'S STORY*

Narrator Simon was brought in as a third-party project management consultant to help with project communication issues on a multisite, international project.

Context A multinational project involving work in the UK and the Middle East. The project was to install equipment on two sites and process products between those two sites.

Issue Planning schedules was a nightmare. The UK site had shop-floor staff working three eight-hour shifts five days a week (Monday to Friday) and management staff working between 9 am and 6 pm (Monday to Friday). The Middle East sites had staff working between 6 am and 2 pm (Saturday to Wednesday).

Solution Simon created a unique project schedule which took into account the different staff work timetables in the UK and also the different work dates in the Middle East. He also recommended appointing a sub-project manager for the Middle Eastern part of the project, who was aware of the working patterns there but could also communicate easily with the UK.

Learning Having a single time frame for the project that took into account three different work schedules made life easier to plan. Having a local manager in the Middle East made communication a lot easier – although the sub-project manager was under a lot of pressure and ended up working very odd hours!

So just what is project management? – frequently asked questions

The following table provides quick answers to some of the most fre-quently asked questions about project management. Use this as a way of gaining a quick overview.

FAQ 1 Where do I start?	1 Often people feel overwhelmed when initially presented with a project. If you have used a methodology or process previously, then ask yourself whether you found it useful or whether it worked for you. If it is appropriate, use the same approach. The starting point is often to really understand the business need, rather than the first activities within the project. Ask the key stakeholder why the project is necessary and what they are hoping to achieve. Once you understand this, you can get more involved with activity.
FAQ 2 Do I have to get a project management qualification?	2 Absolutely not! A lot of project management qualifications are very, very intensive and geared towards full-time, specialist project managers in a certain area or discipline. In our experience most project managers have a 'day job' as well as the management of a project. Get some core project skills and techniques under your belt rather than getting a full qualification. Later on, when you are more experienced, you may want to get qualified.
FAQ 3 How many objectives should my project have?	3 It depends. What are you trying to achieve? Too many objectives and they could become contradictory, too few and there is a risk that your project does not deliver enough value. There is no set number but you need to ensure that the business needs are met. There should be a direct link between the business needs and the project objectives.
FAQ 4 To whom should I go for support?	4 Formally, you should have a project sponsor. Their role is to ensure that the rest of the business supports you and your project. In addition, a project review board (PRB) may be available to listen to your comments and answers to questions about the progress of the project. If you are new to project management, then get yourself a mentor to help you with certain project management techniques and answer your questions.

FAQ 5 *What's the value of stakeholder analysis?*	5 This is a relatively new phenomenon in project management, which recognises that even the best-planned projects may fail if they do not get the support of the key people 'behind the scenes'. Spend some time at the beginning of a project thinking through who could accelerate or kill off your project if they so wanted. These are the key stakeholders and you need to keep them on your side. Remember, if there is a sniff of success about your project, then everybody will want to be involved.
FAQ 6 *How do I get the right people in my project team?*	6 Your core project team will help determine success. In terms of getting the right people, you might want to look at a balance between experience and new people with new ideas. In the projects we have managed we often look for a balance of skills – including those with technical experience of planning and executing the project, as well as those with excellent communication and 'people' skills. As contract project managers, coming into a company's project from outside, we would look for a team that can complement our skills, not duplicate them. We look for those people who have knowledge of the subject matter rather than technical planning skills. Only you will know whether the right balance has been struck.
FAQ 7 *Do I need to know how to use the Microsoft Project application?*	7 It is people who run projects, not software. Undoubtedly some project software can be a real benefit, but some very complex and sizeable projects have been successfully delivered using a spreadsheet and Post-it notes! Learn to use a manual technique first, and then see if software can help. You may need someone to manage the data production, but focus on the outcomes rather than the tool you use.
FAQ 8 *Do I plan from the start or from the projected finish of my project?*	8 Research shows that most people seem to plan from the projected end point of the project. This is sometimes known as the 'backward pass' technique. Start from an end point, plan activities and resources, and then put in a projected start date. The start date you will come up with is probably half a year ago, so this is where the fun of 'crunching' your project plan starts!
FAQ 9 *Are all my activities part of a project?*	9 'To a man with a hammer, everything looks like a nail!' Once you have some experience in managing projects, there is a temptation to use the technique on all and every task laid before you. Ask yourself: 'Do I need to sit down and

plan this in detail?' If the honest answer is 'No', then don't overcomplicate things. Use your judgement in deciding the detail required. Think about who is going to use your plan and how.

FAQ 10 What are the most crucial techniques in project management?

10 Project management is a huge subject area. There are many tools and techniques that you can use and it is difficult to come up with the crucial few. However, it is often best not to start project activities until you know the following:
→ Who is the project sponsor and are they enthusiastic?
→ What are the agreed objectives?
→ Has a project plan been calculated?

FAQ 11 In project planning, how do I know that I have remembered everything?

11 There is no foolproof way to ensure that nothing has been forgotten. History is full of projects that forgot crucial elements until the last minute. Use the project team, sponsors and stakeholders to help you plan. Ask yourself: 'If we complete all the activities, will we meet the project's objectives?' Learn from previous similar projects.

FAQ 12 How do I stop scope creep?

12 Here are some suggestions to help you avoid scope creep:
→ Understand the business need and get key stakeholders to sign off the objectives.
→ Make all objectives SMART: specific, measurable, agreed, realistic and time bound (see page 41).
→ Have a clear change control process, with formal sign-off for changes.
→ Manage all issues and potential changes through regular meetings.
→ Communicate, communicate, communicate.

FAQ 13 If a project is running off track, how do I kill it before it does damage?

13 Using a stage-gate process is possibly the best way of ensuring that a project with the potential to go off course can be stopped quickly and easily. Break your project into phases (stages), and between each phase have decision-making meetings (gates). Review progress at each gate and decide 'Go', 'No Go', 'Hold' or 'Kill'. Have clear criteria at each stage gate.

FAQ 14 There is a 'review cycle' as part of my project – how many 'cycles' should I plan for in my project?

14 The risk here is that you review too many times, with the project running over budget and time. Based on research and prior learning, agree in advance how many 'cycles' you will plan for: cost and time those in advance. For example, a client was creating a news-sheet for publication. He had planned on three editorial cycles, that is, editing the copy, sending back for corrections and amendments. He knew that on average each cycle took a week and added £2,000 to the project in terms of staff costs. If the three cycles were exceeded, then he might have to go

with what he had got or kill off the project. In fact, after two editorial cycles most work was good enough, and he therefore went ahead with it. The project budget was underspent and he had even 'gained' a week, too.

FAQ 15 *I have no project budget – how do I go about calculating one?*

15 As early as possible in the planning phase, use tools like the responsibility assignment matrix (RAM) and the resources matrix (see page 58) to break down resource requirements to the level at which you can start costing tasks and pieces of work. These are simply matrices listing those involved in doing tasks across the top and the project plan down the side. They can detail the resources required or the skills necessary for each task. Use them to add up the costs and assess potential risks, and then use this information as the basis for budgeting.

FAQ 16 *My project is complex; do I have to break it down into every single activity?*

16 Delegate where possible. Agree on an overall structure to the project and where possible delegate the creation of a work breakdown structure (WBS) to relevant managers and specialists. However, you and your core team will have to bring all the WBS parts together, so check for duplication, look for synergies and efficiency savings, and then create a master WBS.

FAQ 17 *What tools can I use in creating a WBS?*

17 A spreadsheet is as useful as any specialist software. In fact the Post-It® note is also invaluable for creating an overall structure and outline to the project and is very flexible in breaking a WBS into its constituent parts. Make sure you understand the process of creating a WBS and project planning before investing in specialist software.

FAQ 18 *How much detail is required in the WBS?*

18 You have to weigh up the risks of under-planning against the costs of over-planning. The creation of a WBS is an iterative process: go over it several times until you are happy that everything is covered to the level you, as project manager, are happy with. There is no simple answer here, so getting experienced assistance will help.

QUICK TIP *SCHEDULING*

Start non-critical tasks as early as resources will allow, to free up resources later.

FAQ 19 Where do I put in milestones?	**19** Wherever and whenever you want to check progress against plan, put a milestone into the project schedule and coordinate a review meeting at that point. Be careful not to have too many review meetings: make the milestone meetings 'event'-oriented rather than on a regular schedule. Put them at critical points or phases in the project.
FAQ 20 How do I get people to turn up to an end-of-project review?	**20** If people are looking forward to the next project, or if the project was not a great success, there will be a reluctance to attend an end-of-project review. Make the review informal – if you serve beer and pizzas and use it as a chance to thank people as well as review performance, people may be more inclined to attend! A key principle is that the project team should look to learn before, during and after each project.

We hope that these FAQs give a quick start to getting to grips with project management. The rest of this book shows you how to move from understanding what the key elements of project management are to an active implementation of project management within your team, department or across the company.

Managing in complexity – project management as practical wisdom

Dr Svetlana Cicmil

Given the highly complex nature of projects and the project management task, it is relevant to ask questions about the degree to which a rational approach to decision making will achieve the desired outcomes. Much of the thinking and writing about project management has emphasised the use of tools and techniques and a 'scientific' or instrumental approach to the task. It would be easy for the newly appointed project manager to make assumptions about the power of a technocratic approach in shaping projects and the project environment. My research[1] is

[1] Cicmil, S. and Marshall, D. (2005), 'Insights into collaboration at project level: complexity, social interaction and procurement mechanisms', *Building Research and Information*, 33(6), 523–35; Cicmil, S. (2006), 'Understanding project management practice through interpretative and critical research perspectives', *Project Management Journal*, 37(2), 27–37.

EXPERT VOICE

focused around the question posed by many starting a project manage-ment career: 'What does it mean to be, or take to become, an expert or virtuoso project manager?'

In the course of my research I have developed a framework of the com-plexity of projects and project environments that enables the exploration of how project managers cope with complexity in practice, how they think in action and what kind of knowledge, skills and competencies they find useful in accomplishing their project management tasks and responsibilities. I have identified three key interrelated concerns, which call for a range of alternative skills for coping with and responding to the challenges in project environ-ments. These concerns result from the fact that projects do not follow a neat pre-planned pathway. The initial plans get influenced by the evolution, emer-gence and radical unpredictability of the outcomes of decisions, actions and interactions among project participants, as well as by the impact of technol-ogy during the project's life. The three interrelated themes of project complexity are:

1 **Criteria and measurement of project performance.** This concern is part of project-related decision making from a conception and approval stage, when the project proposal is evaluated against its prospective, expected or desired benefits. Because we all have only limited decision-making capability in our thought processes, if we are confronted with time and information limitations then we tend to reduce the overall complexity of the problem or challenge to some-thing with which we can cope. This is described as a process of 'bounded rationality'. In a project, there is a complex interplay between often multiple and conflicting agendas and understandings of technology, and success and risks, among diverse decision makers and project stakeholders. This all results in ambiguity and the equivocality of set project goals, key performance indicators and project success/failure criteria, which then continue throughout the project life cycle. Multiple perspectives are always present on all project issues, where gain and loss often depend on the perspec-tive taken by the stakeholder in question. Coping with the resulting tension between rationality and power requires individual and institu-tional transparency and accountability. It also needs contractual and institutional checks and balances, driven by performance-enhancing possibilities through participation and future-oriented options rather than by explicit rules governing practices. Ultimately, a helicopter view, an integrative perspective, sound judgement in decision making and the willingness to act in the face of these uncertainties marks out the effective project manager.

2 **Inherent unpredictability of future events affecting the project**. People's actions, responses and behaviour during project work, as well as changes in technology, expectations and a wider environment affecting project participants and stakeholders, always induce a degree of apprehension in what acting 'professionally' means in the circumstances of 'not knowing' exactly what is coming next. This exposes shortcomings of a dominant 'control' paradigm of project management and its understanding as a technical discipline driven by the assumption of the possibility of detailed planning and prediction. The notion of time-flux accounts for long-planning horizons, implying inevitable change of scope and ambition over time among multiple project parties. This calls for project control that is not just structurally formalised through contracts clauses, penalties and law, but also socialised through participation and collaboration among participants. In this way it becomes possible for the project manager to deal simultaneously with both project implementation (i.e. ensuring that the required work is being accomplished) and direction (facilitating joint action required for project completion) when there is no value equilibrium. Consequently, the distinguishing feature of project managers is not control, but the ability to operate effectively in an ambiguous environment. It is also the ability individually and collectively to maintain their sense of self and their defences against uncertainty in order to create a collaborative atmosphere in which further joint action is possible towards accomplishing the project.

3 **Multi-agency interfaces**. Social interaction and processes of relating among project actors (project promoters, funding bodies, public, law representatives, contractors, etc.) with different professional backgrounds, cultures, logics of representation, value systems and positions of power are complex. During the project's life, over time, these interactions change and will simultaneously be changed by power asymmetries, collaborative intentions, emotions, resistance, micro-diversity, collective learning and identity-change processes. But, because projects are social settings in which people accomplish their tasks not only by performing their job competently but also by interacting with each other, the progress of work as well as the control of project implementation is embedded in and created by this very micro-diversity in the project setting. Good project management therefore is about understanding the potential as well as the complexity of this micro-diversity and relationships over time, and capitalising on that understanding in order to accomplish the project. This requires the project manager to be

sensitive to the patterns of conversational, cultural and power-relating that go on in a given project, and to be prepared to engage and participate creatively in these processes of interaction. Conversational skills and self-awareness are needed for the project manager to secure the emergence of collaborative action to enable the 'next step' and create a position from which further actions, acceptable to them and other project actors, are possible.

Managing in complexity, i.e. coping simultaneously with unpredictability, change, continuous renegotiation of goals, anxiety and risk, while actiing creatively in the moments of 'dislocation' (not knowing, not being in control) outlined above requires many skills. These include:

→ The ability to pay attention to the quality of conversations that enable action (conversational skills for persuasion, renegotiation of original promises and plans, maintaining encouragement, motivation and confidence, etc.) in the environment where there is a high level of diversity and tension between agendas, interests or values.

→ The capacity to use both rhetoric (facilitating conversations by introducing 'persuasive themes' that encourage new patterns of behaviour and relating) and technical or control devices (contracts, plans, report documents).

→ A good enough control of anxiety when facing unpredictability, with an ability to 'think on one's feet'.

→ A deep understanding of a project's micro-diversity – both its destructive and constructive potential – and an ability to build alliances and supportive collegiate networks.

→ A sensitivity to one's own action and self-awareness in the environments where multiple value systems and asymmetries of power have emerged under particular historic and social circumstances, often creating 'winners and losers'.

→ The ability to face as well as to exercise power.

These proposed skills of an expert project manager embrace intuition, judgement and social and political virtuosity in local contexts. They can be sharply contrasted with the mainstream, conventional prescriptions for 'best practice' in project management, which promote a more instrumental, technical kind of expert knowledge. The project manager's daily job (monitoring, control, replanning, reporting, communication with stakeholders, decision making) should be seen as social and political action guided by a context-dependent skill: an ability to think and act by transparently acknowledging and deliberating about values and interests in the context and by encouraging dialogue and voices from different project groups in deciding on the project direction. This is a move beyond the limited perception of project managers as skilful technicians, and requires innovative and creative models of management development and education, acknowledging the role of experience and self-reflection in creating the kind of well-rounded, social competence of project managers, outlined above. ""

PROJECT MANAGEMENT AUDIT

In order to improve performance you first need to understand what your starting point is, what your strengths and weaknesses are and how each will promote or limit what you can achieve. There are two levels of awareness you need to have. The first is to understand what the most effective teams or businesses, in terms of project management, look like and behave and how near your team is to emulating them. The second is to understand what it takes to lead such a team – do you personally have the necessary attributes for success?

Team assessment

Is my team maximising its potential to manage projects?

Use the following checklist to assess the current state of your team, considering each element in turn. Use a simple Red-Amber-Green evaluation, where Red reflects areas where you feel strongly that the statement is not correct in your organisation and suggests there are significant issues requiring immediate attention, Amber suggests areas of concern and risk and Green means that you are happy with your current state.

ID	CATEGORY	EVALUATION CRITERIA	STATUS
Project management			RAG
P1	Business needs	Projects are well aligned to business imperatives and reflect customer and consumer needs; interdependencies with other projects are highlighted	☐
P2	Project goals	All projects have clear objectives with agreed key performance indicators (KPIs) and targets, and each has established a business case or return on investment	☐
P3	Stakeholders	Key stakeholders are identified and their commitment assessed; teams actively plan to take action to win over resisters	☐
P4	Workplan and timings	Tasks and priorities are defined, the critical path identified and milestones agreed	☐
P5	Issues and risks	Issues and risks are identified, corrective actions agreed and change requests managed; contingency plans are in place	☐
P6	The team	Project leaders are selected appropriately and teams are built with clear roles and responsibilities	☐
P7	Critical decisions	Critical decisions are identified, a decision-making process is agreed and buy-in to the resulting decisions is gained from key stakeholders	☐
P8	Resources and budget	Resource requirements are identified and assessed in terms of quantity and quality, and budgets are agreed	☐
P9	Project leadership	The right people are appointed as project sponsors; project leaders have the right skills, right way of thinking and right level of commitment	☐
P10	Communications	A process of communication is agreed that ensures the right information goes to the right stakeholders in the right format at the right time	☐

CASE STORY **CENTRAL GOVERNMENT, GRAHAM'S STORY**

Narrator Graham is a project manager within a central government department on a major infrastructure project (he is a contractor on a long-term contract).

Context In common with other government projects that operate across a number of departments, a steering committee of senior staff had been appointed to oversee progress. This group meets once a month, causing the project team to drop things for half a day to prepare for the meeting, spend half a day in the meeting and another half a day in following up.

Issue The time taken up by these meetings was causing project delay and cost overrun, as well as morale problems among the project leaders and teams.

Solution Graham assigned one person per team to the task of looking after each steering committee. Their job was simple – save project team time. They used only information that the project team was already generating and did not ask for any help in preparation. They got close to members of the committee and used that relationship to shield the teams. They did all the follow-up.

Learning Do not just accept procedures that are counterproductive. You do not necessarily have to take them on and get them changed, but look for a way of reducing the pain on project teams.

Self-assessment

Do I have what it takes?

This section presents a self-assessment checklist of the factors that make a successful Fast Track leader in project management. These reflect the knowledge, competencies, attitudes and behaviours required to get to the top, irrespective of your current level of seniority. Take control of your career, behave professionally and reflect on your personal vision for the next five years. This assessment creates a framework for action throughout the rest of the book.

QUICK TIP REVIEW

Review past projects of a similar nature. Find out the pitfalls and potential risk areas – and also where easy wins can be made.

So, this next section 'audits' you as an individual in the knowledge, competencies, attitudes and behaviours usually associated with success in the leadership and management of projects. Use the checklist on the next page to identify where you personally need to gain knowledge or skills. Fill it in honestly and then get someone who knows you well, your boss or a key member of your team, to go over it with you. Be willing to change your assessment if people give you insights into yourself that you had not taken into account.

Use the following scoring process:

0 A totally new area of knowledge or skills

1 You are aware of the area but have low knowledge and/or lack skills

2 An area where you are reasonably competent and working on improvement

3 An area where you have a satisfactory level of knowledge and skills

4 An area where you are consistently well above average

5 You are recognised as a key figure in this area of knowledge and skills throughout the business

Reflect on the lowest scores and identify those areas that are critical to success. Flag these as status Red, requiring immediate attention. Then identify those areas that you are concerned about and flag those as status Amber, implying areas of development that need to be monitored closely. Status Green implies that you are satisfied with the current state.

ID	CATEGORY	EVALUATION CRITERIA	SCORE	STATUS
Knowledge			0–5	RAG
K1	Industry and markets	I have a deep knowledge of my industry in terms of scope (boundaries), overall size and growth, and major trends. As a result I have a clear understanding of the type of projects that will naturally occur		
K2	Business context	I have a good understanding of where my project(s) fit and link to the business strategy. I make people aware of what they contribute to the long-term growth strategy of the organisation		
K3	Portfolio management	I know how projects relate to each other and understand priorities, resource limitations and potential areas of internal project conflict		
K4	Best practice	I am aware of the latest thinking in project management as a discipline and know about those tools and techniques rated as 'fit for purpose' within my organisation		
Competencies				
C1	Project management	I have the ability to define, plan, monitor and control change activities in order to deliver identified performance improvements on time and within budget		
C2	Risk management	I can think ahead and identify, prioritise and mitigate barriers to effective and enduring implementation within projects		
C3	Decision making	I am proficient at identifying areas for decisions, generating options, understanding the risks of alternatives and communicating decisions to stakeholders		
C4	Communication	I have a high level of skill in communicating high-level visions, objectives and detailed plans to differing project teams as clearly and concisely as possible		

ID	CATEGORY	EVALUATION CRITERIA	SCORE	STATUS
Attitudes			0–5	RAG
A1	Flexibility	I have developed the mindset that if things go astray I seek and act upon other ways of reaching the project objectives	☐	☐
A2	Continual improvement	I learn from past successes and failures and strive to get better and better with each new project	☐	☐
A3	High expectations	I expect the best from all involved in the project and set high professional standards throughout	☐	☐
A4	Results oriented	Achieving the goal, despite setbacks and changes, is uppermost in my mind for the duration of the project. This is linked to remaining flexible in all things	☐	☐
Behaviours				
B1	Directional	I take decisions or risks on my own when appropriate. However, I can be autocratic and controlling if the project faces a crisis and there is no time to consult	☐	☐
B2	Analytical	I insist on detailed facts, observations and analysis to enable the right strategic decisions to be made and risks to be assessed	☐	☐
B3	Opinion seeking	I ask for input and opinions in order to make decisions, so building confidence in teams and individuals and getting buy-in from stakeholders	☐	☐
B4	Democratic	I encourage team participation and involvement and empower team members, to help strengthen commitment to the project	☐	☐

QUICK TIP *PLANNING*
With multiple projects, put them in order of priority as soon as possible, to avoid damaging and costly conflicts later on.

Audit summary

Take a few minutes to reflect on the leadership–team effectiveness matrix below and consider your current position: where are you and what are the implications?

→ **Bottom left – poor leadership and an ineffective team.** This will result in failure: who knows, you may already be too late.

→ **Top left – great leadership but a poor team.** You have a great vision but will be unlikely to implement it, and so it will have little impact. You will need to find a way of taking people with you and introducing systems and processes to improve team effectiveness.

→ **Bottom right – poor leadership but a great team.** You are highly effective and efficient as a team but may well be going in the wrong direction through poor leadership.

→ **Top right – clear leadership and direction combined with an efficient and effective team.** This is where we want to be. Lots of great new ideas for project management linked to current business goals and with a team unit capable of delivering on time and within budget. You don't need this book – please give it to someone else!

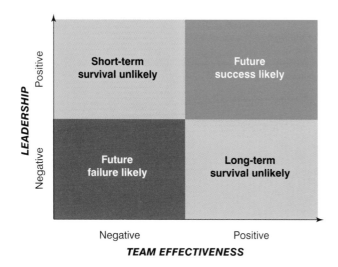

QUICK TIP RESOURCES

Estimate costs carefully. Use estimation techniques when getting many different costings for the same task. Remember that once costs are approved, you are bound by them.

STOP – THINK – ACT

Part A has given you a quick overview of what project management is, and you will also have assessed the performance of yourself and your team against best practice checklists. This will have raised your awareness of what is possible and clarified where you are now.

Take time to reflect on your profile in order to identify any 'quick wins' you could achieve today and to see what chapters of the book could help the most. Look for areas where you could get a 'quick win' and improve matters in the short term. Ask yourself and the team these questions:

What should we do?	What will we change today, and what difference will it make (why)?
Who do we need to involve?	Who else needs to be involved to make it work and why?
What resources will we require?	What information, facilities, materials, equipment or budget will be required and are they available?
What is the timing?	When will this change be implemented – is there a deadline?

Visit www.Fast-Track-Me.com to use the Fast Track online planning tool.

Managing risk on projects
Dr Stephen Simister

There are risks and costs to a program of action. But they are far less than the long-range risks and costs of comfortable inaction. (John F. Kennedy)

Projects are undertaken in order to realise opportunity. Risk is present in all projects. Hence, projects are a balance of risk and opportunity. A high-risk project will have to yield a high level of opportunity to make the project worthwhile. The challenge for project management is to reduce the risk while maximising the opportunity. My focus here is on risk.[1]

Project managers are routinely involved in making decisions that have a major impact on risk. In practice, many key project decisions are taken, consciously or otherwise, to mitigate risk. But risk management is concerned with establishing a formal set of processes and practices by which risk is managed, rather than being dealt with by default. The effective management of risk, while the responsibility of project management, can only be achieved by the actions of the whole project team, including the client.

Risk management is a process for identifying, assessing and responding to risks associated with delivering an objective – for example, constructing a new office building – and the focus here is on commercial-type risks. Health and safety-related risks are likely to need separate consideration and are outside the scope of this discussion. Risk management formalises the intuitive approach to risk that project teams often undertake. By utilising a formal approach, project teams can manage risk in a more proactive manner, shaping and moulding the future state of a project. In addition, there needs to be an overall risk management strategy so that this risk management process is implemented in a coordinated fashion. This strategy should include how risk management will be integrated into the project management process throughout the project's life cycle.

Risk management should be flexible, adapting to the circumstances of the client's needs and the project. Some clients require a snapshot of the risks at the outset of the project, with an initial risk assessment, the provision of a one-off risk register and a quick estimate of the combined effect. Other projects may require a full risk management service, with risk being continually addressed throughout the project.

Risk management should be undertaken as part of a structured, formal process that needs to be aligned to the overall approach to project management. These are the key elements that need to be considered as part of a risk management process:

→ Identify staff and resources that will be involved in the risk management process.

→ Define lines of reporting and responsibility for the risk management process.

[1] Further information can be found in Simister, S. J. (2004), 'Qualitative and quantitative risk management' in P.W.G. Morris and J.K. Pinto (eds), *The Wiley Guide to Managing Projects*, Hoboken, NJ: Wiley. For opportunity management see Hillson, D. (2008), *Effective Opportunity Management for Projects: Exploiting Positive Risk*, Abingdon: Marcel Dekker.

EXPERT VOICE

→ Link the risk management plan to other project management tools, such as safety, quality and environmental management, and planning and reporting systems.

→ Consolidate all risks identified into an appropriate and digestible response strategy, in order that cumulative effects can be perceived.

→ State risk audit intervals and key milestones.

→ Include risk milestones in project plans.

→ Identify possible response strategies and programmes for each risk category, including contingency plans and how to handle new or unresolved risks.

→ Assess the costs involved.

→ Monitor the success of responses strategies and produce feedback for reporting into future projects.

The management of risk is such a key element in any project that the project manager needs not only to be knowledgeable about the process but also to be proactive in examining and monitoring risks throughout the lifetime of the project. Part of good decision-making practice is clearly to assess the risk as part of the decision-making process, but it is often given scant attention. An important consideration for the project manager is that of recognising when to call in experts to ensure that the approach is sound. The potential downside of poor risk management is the impact not only on project success but also on realising new opportunities by undertaking future projects. Appropriately, Sir Winston Churchill said: 'The pessimist sees difficulty in every opportunity. The optimist sees the opportunity in every difficulty'.

PART B

BUSINESS
FAST TRACK

I rrespective of your chosen function or discipline, look around at the successful managers who you know and admire. We call these people Fast Track managers, people who have the knowledge and skills to perform well and fast track their careers. Notice how they excel at three things:

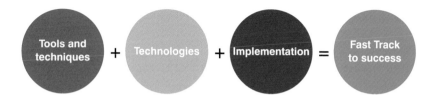

Tools and techniques

They have a good understanding of best practices for their particular field. This is in the form of methods and techniques that translate knowledge into decisions, insights and actions. They understand what the best companies do and have an ability to interpret what is relevant for their own businesses. The processes they use are generally simple to explain and form a logical step-by-step approach to solving a problem or capturing data and insights. They also encourage creativity – Fast Track managers do not follow a process slavishly where they know they are filling in the boxes rather than looking for insights on how to improve performance. This combination of method and creativity produces the optimum solutions.

They also have a clear understanding of what is important to know and what is simply noise. They either know this information or have it at their fingertips as and when they require it. They also have effective filtering mechanisms so that they don't get overloaded with extraneous information. The level of detail required varies dramatically from one situation to another – the small entrepreneur will work a lot more on the knowledge they have and in gaining facts from quick conversations with experts, whereas a large corporate may employ teams of analysts and research companies. Frequently when a team is going through any process they uncover the need for further data.

Technologies

However, having the facts and understanding best practice will achieve little unless they are built into the systems that people use on a day-to-day basis. Fast Track managers are good at assessing the relevance of new information technologies and adopting the appropriate ones in order to maximise both effectiveness and efficiency.

Implementation

Finally, having designed the framework that is appropriate to them and their team, Fast Track managers have strong influencing skills and are also great at leading the implementation effort, putting in place the changes necessary to build and sustain the performance of the team.

How tightly or loosely you will use the various tools and techniques presented in Part B will vary, and will to a certain extent depend on personal style. As you read through the following three chapters, first seek to understand how each could impact you and your team, and then decide what level of change may be appropriate given your starting point, authority and career aspirations.

FAST TRACK TOP TEN

This chapter presents a framework of methods or techniques to improve performance and make life as a new project manager easier. Each function can take a lifetime to master, but the Fast Track manager will know which areas to focus on – get those areas right and the chances of success improve. Often success relates to the introduction of simple tools and techniques to improve effectiveness and efficiency.

Introducing project management tools and techniques

What needs to be included? – the top ten tools and techniques?

There are literally thousands of tools and techniques available to the project manager in all areas of project management. Some tools and techniques are so esoteric and specialised that only a few project managers in the country might ever use them, and even then only rarely. Other techniques might only be relevant to certain types of projects. So, which ones to pick?

The criteria for selection in our top ten is based on two elements: those included in our integrated project management framework and those we have used ourselves on client projects and think will be useful to you, the reader, in the majority of projects in which you may be involved. As you gain experience in project management there will be certain techniques and approaches that will become your 'favourites' and will define your 'style' and approach to management. The integrated project management framework can be seen as your 'project strategy' or process, designed to help in all projects that you manage (see figure).

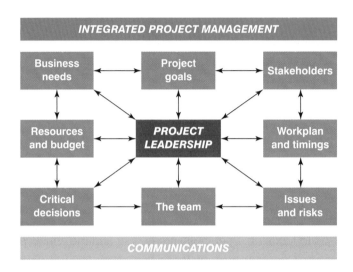

1 Always remembering that projects are a means of delivering value to an organisation, it is worth starting with the **business needs** section and looking at how to create a *project SPRINT*.

2 **Project goals** are closely aligned to business needs, and therefore how to set clear *objectives* is a good skill to possess.

3 Next we will look at **stakeholders** and *stakeholder analysis* as a technique, emphasising the importance of keeping all key players 'on side'.

4 In the section on **workplan and timings** there are many techniques to choose from, but we have decided to concentrate on *critical path* analysis and calculation as a central tool.

5 In **issues and risks** a simple technique for *planning contingencies* has always proved useful and can be used for each and every project.

6 In **the team** we look at *selecting* the best people for the job and defining their roles and function.

7 Linked in with this team working, we look at how to make **critical decisions** within projects.

8 Again, there are many tools and techniques for managing **resources and budget** but a simple way of creating a *project budget* and planning resources is always useful.

9 In terms of **project leadership**, knowing when and when not to *delegate* is often a key success factor and something that those new to project management may struggle with.

10 Finally, understanding what project **communications** are all about and how to establish a *communication plan* are always useful, whatever the project.

 CASE STORY *INTERNATIONAL BANK, PATRICK'S STORY*

Narrator Patrick was working as a consultant with a US-based bank to improve project delivery and to track project progress.

Context Projects were underresourced and consequently failed to deliver stated benefits and meet business objectives within budget.

Issue The bank had a lack of clarity on the overall project portfolio. Middle management was hard-pressed to keep all the projects running to time and there was a feeling that senior management were unsure of the size and scale of the project portfolio.

Solution Having reviewed the differing perceptions of the scale and scope of the project portfolio, Patrick discovered that senior management had underestimated the number of projects underway by a factor of three. Following his review, it was decided that the organisation needed to install a web-based project tool to give all parties concerned a view of both the number and the scope of the projects in the portfolio. Additionally, the new tool meant that project managers were able to flag issues and concerns to the senior team instantly.

Learning Without full visibility and control over the portfolio the role of a project manager is made more difficult by poor senior management decisions. Understanding your total number of projects in hand and their link to corporate strategy is a necessary prerequisite for effective resource allocation and management.

1 BUSINESS NEEDS The value of a SPRINT

It must always be remembered that projects are there to deliver value to the organisation. In lengthy and complex projects the people involved sometimes simply lose sight of why they are doing what they are doing. Seeing the bigger picture allows those involved in managing and delivering projects to be as flexible as possible at all times, without, however, losing the focus on the needs of the business.

For example, we once worked with a very large German chemicals company which was in the midst of spinning off its 'speciality chemicals' division to a banking-led consortium. There was, therefore, pressure to generate value in that division to get the best price it could. As such, the company was focused on getting as many projects (new products) to completion as possible within a fairly short timescale. The project managers and the project management office (PMO) were consummate professionals who did things according to their book. They were obsessed with 'doing things right' in their own inimical style.

However, a third of the way through a major project, producing a new chemical, competitors launched a similar product. In this sector, first to market is everything, so the best thing would have been to review the business need and decide whether the project could be amended or cancelled. However, because the focus was on 'doing things right', the project continued and the product (well made and excellently project-managed) was brought to market on time, within budget and to the required specification.

The competitors had, however, stolen a march on the chemicals company and its product failed to sell. It was clear that the focus should have been on the business need and 'doing the right thing' (i.e. changing or killing the project) rather than on the detail of managing a project excellently – 'doing things right'.

In many organisations people involved are not always even informed as to what the project is about, from a business perspective. They are told what to do and when to do it and possibly even the quality standard pertaining to their task in hand, but they are not given the big picture. If you, as a manager, believe that people will give of their best when asked to achieve something and that your role is to motivate and inspire them, communicating the bigger picture and getting people to understand the business need is crucial.

QUICK TIP OBJECTIVES
Be prepared to drop objectives that have a low priority in order to help manage resources. Your focus should always be on the primary objective.

One of the best ways of ensuring that all projects deliver the value required by a business is to use a checklist so that you do not miss out anything when defining the scope of the project. This checklist ensures that:

→ you avoid duplication and gaps in the overall project or programme;

→ your project addresses the real need and not what people think has got to happen;

→ team members have a common understanding of how the project will deliver value (a common agreed understanding is known to be a necessary prerequisite for team building and the creation of commitment).

One of the most useful checklists at this level is SPRINT. This acronym stands for situation, problem (or opportunity), risks, impact, needs and timing.

Taking every opportunity to build team spirit and commitment, it may be worth getting your core project team together to help go through the SPRINT checklist and then double-checking this with the project sponsor. The core project team in most cases consists of, as a minimum, you, the project manager, your deputy, any sub-project managers and specialists involved for the duration of the project and a representative of the project sponsor or key stakeholder. The SPRINT checklist should help them understand what the project is about. It may be the case that some of these business questions or answers have been created in a brief from the project sponsor or senior management team. In this case, ensure that all key project staff understand what is in that brief and take the time to go back to the source and ask any clarifying questions. Time spent at this early stage in clarifying the business needs is time well spent.

→ **Situation.** This is the business situation that necessitates your project. Frame the working of the situation in such a way that all involved in the project can understand it in the context of the project and the organisation's goals. It could be a simple statement such as, 'With high PC ownership in Germany there is an opportunity to open up online shopping.' It could also be the results of a business review recommending specific actions such as, 'Open an online retail presence in German as part of our expansion into Europe.' In any case, the situation needs to be as clear and unambiguous as possible. The stimulus for the situation statement can come from many sources, such as a political decision or a review of the economic situation, but it needs to be brief, to the point and clear to all.

→ **Problem (or opportunity).** What is the problem that the business is facing, or what opportunities are there that the project aims to exploit? These questions allow people to be more flexible and add value to the project as it progresses. The problem could be a statement such as, 'We are not exploiting our website for selling purposes,' or restated as an opportunity: 'Develop the website in order to maximise European online sales opportunities.' Obviously, the problem or the opportunity relates to the situation statement.

→ **Risks.** These are the risks of *not* doing the project. Don't confuse these risks with the project risks, which we will deal with later. Do not over-hype the risks, or the credibility of the project is put at stake, but do demonstrate that if the organisation does not do something about the problem or opportunity there will possibly be adverse ramifications. This could be as simple as stating, 'European sales teams will become demotivated and lose potential bonuses if we do not provide online shopping tools for their customers.'

→ **Impact.** What will be the quantified impact on the bottom line performance of the business? This is a quantitative assessment of the problem and risks. Some people need figures to help them understand issues, while other people may be more influenced by emotive arguments instead. For example, 'Online shopping in Germany, in our sector, is forecast to grow by €20 million in the next three years. This equates to 30 per cent of our entire growth target.'

→ **Needs.** Based on an assessment of the issues the business faces, what is the need or requirement? What is the purpose of the project? The answers to these two questions must link directly to the project's objectives. For example, 'To improve our online e-tailing offer to the German-speaking market and support expansion into Europe with new websites and portals.'

→ **Timing.** What are the deadlines for satisfying the needs? These should link into the *project statement* and later on into the objectives. A project statement is a single sentence that states what the project is to deliver, by when and within what budget or costs. For example, 'Our German subsidiary needs to have a European online presence by the end of the financial year created within a budget of €200,000.'

It may be impossible to gather all the SPRINT information in one go – for example, at a meeting with all sponsors and the project team. In reality, you will probably acquire it over a period of time in smaller meetings before the project starts in earnest. If this is not feasible, you can always allocate what is missing in the project statement to other senior project members and then complete it later.

2 PROJECT GOALS *Setting clear objectives*

Essential ingredients for success in project management include defined and agreed goals, a committed team and a viable and flexible plan of action. To achieve your goals, ensure that these essentials are in place. Once you have communicated a vision to the sponsor and team, perhaps using SPRINT, it is time to set clear objectives. Objectives are there to measure the progress and ultimately the success of the project and to support any Go/No Go decisions.

Not all projects have a 'vision statement', but if your project does, you should use this as the basis for explaining what your project is going to do. There is always a degree of interpretation in a vision statement and therefore project objectives should always be checked with the project sponsor and key stakeholders to get consensus on them before you start the implementation. The vision should reflect, for example, the relative importance of time, cost and performance within your project. For instance, 'time to market' might be the prime driver even at the expense of product functionality or cost – 'To have the software available by end of next quarter' may override 'To have five new functions available within a budget of £200,000'.

How do you ensure that project objectives are clear and valid?

→ **List the objectives you wish to achieve or have elicited from the vision statement.**

→ **Try to avoid listing an activity instead of an objective.** For example, 'Complete a pilot' does not really answer the question 'Why?' Instead 'Complete a pilot to demonstrate that the project will achieve its planned business impact with minimal risk of spoiling the market' is an objective rather than an action.

→ **Try to make the objectives measurable.** If you are having difficulty with this, then ask yourself: 'How will we know that we have achieved this objective?'

→ **The objectives will probably be debated by a number of people.** Therefore use them as a 'straw man' to discuss with key stakeholders what the project is about and what the objectives should be.

Making objectives SMART

SMART is an acronym that has become very popular with individuals wishing to set clear objectives. However, while many people know what the acronym stands for (or variants thereof), few actually understand what that actually means to the objectives in question. Here, we define the SMART acronym as:

→ **Specific.** So what does specific mean when it comes to setting objectives? For many it means separating multiple objectives out into individual ones and making them detailed and clear. Linking objectves to the business need also ensures that they are specific.

→ **Measurable.** Putting a figure on something makes it easier to measure, but this in itself causes some issues for the project manager. Generally, most objectives are either quantitative or qualitative by nature. Objectives that measure time, cost and outputs tend to be quantitative and therefore not subjective. There is usually a common understanding of these types of objective and the way in which they are measured (the metrics). However, a problem arises when qualitative, subjective elements are included in objectives. Then there needs to be a common understanding of the qualities these objectives are trying to measure and how to measure them. The study of quality management has generated many ways of 'measuring' quality, but for the new project manager the rule seems to be – get a common understanding beforehand of what is meant by 'quality'. If the project requires an objective to be about something that is difficult to put a figure on – for example, happiness, user-friendliness or motivation – ask stakeholders why these qualities are important and how they would know at the end of the project whether they have been achieved.

Some managers categorically insist that if an objective cannot be measured then it has no place as a project objective – it is not 'objective'. Others point to the fact that not all projects are as cut and dried as that and some subjectivity has to be part of the project to add value. The trap that both proponents can fall into is that they end up spending more time setting up a means to measure the objectives and performance than is wise – and ironically end up reducing the actual value of the project.

→ **Agreed**. A fundamental prerequisite for focusing a team and getting it to pull together is a common, agreed, objective. Therefore, in most variants of the SMART acronym 'agreed' has a key part to play. This requires the objectives to be understood by all the stakeholders after a degree of discussion and debate. Ultimately, all concerned must agree to the objectives in order to get the full commitment of people and resources within the team and other stakeholders outside.

→ **Realistic**. For a project to be achievable, the objectives must be realistic. But how do you know whether something is realistic or not? For most project managers, something is realistic when the following are taken into account. Only when you have assessed all the factors below and found them to be positive can the objective be said to be 'realistic':

1 Time – is there enough time to get the project done?

2 Resources – is there a budget and resources (including having the necessary skills and knowledge) to do the job?

3 Other commitments – what else are project managers and key resources committed to?

→ **Time bound**. To drive performance, all objectives should have a deadline associated with them. These should be linked to the other SMART elements and also linked to the project statement. For example, a cutting edge UK manufacturer of domestic appliances, with over 10 per cent of its workforce dedicated to development projects based on its patented approach to cleaning, managed to bring only one new product to market in seven years. It managed to produce over 28 variants of its existing technology and products, but it was always seen as a 'one-trick pony'. On analysing why this was the case, it was found that the founder and CEO was unable to stop tinkering with the technical objectives of projects under-way and therefore 'scope creep' became almost endemic. A bad project should be stopped as soon as possible, but it is almost an equal crime to keep moving the goalposts of a good project in a constant attempt to make things better.

There are many other ways of setting, categorising and detailing project objectives and many debates about, for example, the number of objec-tives any project should have. However, for the Fast Track project manager the SMART tool can put the project on a good footing. Time spent on getting project objectives right is time well spent and will bene-fit the project manager towards the end of the project.

QUICK TIP **OBJECTIVES**
Ask colleagues to read and review your project goals and don't be afraid to go back to stakeholders or the project review board and question them up front.

3 STAKEHOLDERS *Stakeholder analysis*

Talking through many a project 'war story' with project managers, we are always surprised when the matter of 'office politics' raises its head with a project being 'killed off' due to someone 'not liking it' or it 'clashing with their interests'. After many years of hearing this we wondered whether there is anything a project manager could do to offset the risk of a proj-ect clashing with the 'vested interest' within a business. Stakeholder analysis was the answer.

Stakeholder analysis is a name that can be ascribed to a series of tech-niques whose aim is to understand the key players involved in the business environment and their attitude towards your project. Traditionally, we had always thought of stakeholders as being generally either positive or benign towards projects. However, working with the NHS showed Simon how not all stakeholders can be seen as positive and, as such, steps need to be taken well in advance to understand these 'negative' stakeholders and do something accordingly.

QUICK TIP STAKEHOLDERS

Take every opportunity to build a good rapport with your main stakeholders through good communication and regular updates. They hold the key to success and can make life easier for you.

The table below is a simple and straightforward way of assessing key stakeholders' attitudes towards your project.

NAME	ROLE	POWER (HIGH/ MEDIUM/ LOW)	SUPPORT (–5 TO +5)	STATUS RAG	ACTIONS
Ian Smitt	Finance director	High	–5	R	Meet with him as early as possible to understand financial implications of the project. Try to assess budgetary worries and get MD's involvement to help in this area
Toni Ring	MD	High	+5	G	Use him to get senior management team on board as early as possible in the planning process and get a 1-2-1 talk with FD to focus upon financial implications of the project
Gill Mance	IT director	Medium	0	A	Could be useful to get him involved, especially to influence suppliers and contractors. Need to increase support for the project
Sam Bruce	Chairman	High	+1	A	Broadly positive but more support required if the long-term aspects of the project are to be safeguarded and the benefits sold to the rest of the group

NAME	ROLE	POWER (HIGH/ MEDIUM/ LOW)	SUPPORT (–5 TO+5)	STATUS RAG	ACTIONS
Kath Williams	Purchasing and supply chain manager	Low	–2	R	Needs to be sold on the long-term benefits of the project and her fears of redundancies removed. Needs to be involved in detailed objectives and benefits planning

In the first column you name the key stakeholders and in the second their role or function. You then have to assess how much influence or 'power' the individual has within the organisation and over your project especially. In this example we have rated power high, medium or low, but you can score them from 1 to 10 instead.

In the next column you need to gauge their support for your project and its objectives. By support we don't necessarily mean being positive. The support scores go from –5 (i.e. absolutely against your project, its objectives and probably you as the project manager too) to 0 (i.e. neutral to the project, with no strong feelings either way) and through to +5 (i.e. absolute advocate and enthusiast for your project and what it will do).

The status column summarises the power/support axes and high-lights those areas in red which require immediate action or careful planning as to how the individual should be approached. The actions column specifically lists what needs to happen and how to approach an individual. This is the key element of the matrix – not what the relative power and support scores are but what you as a project manager and your core team are going to do about those key stakeholders who have high influence and are dead set against your project.

How to use stakeholder analysis

In a word – carefully. This is one of the few documents that should be closely guarded and restricted to the core project team only. Because we are dealing here with individual attitudes and feelings, stakeholder analysis must be dealt with very carefully and thought through in advance. Some people prefer to remove names from the matrix and put in letters instead to make the technique anonymous.

A French industrial manufacturer we once worked with refused even to contemplate using stakeholder analysis as it was judged to be too 'politically sensitive' in their culture. The irony was that the politics within this company were responsible for delaying and stopping many a project, yet sitting down and assessing why and who was responsible was not judged to be acceptable.

Carry out the stakeholder analysis at the very start of the project, while formulating and discussing objectives. It should link to the communication plan and consider how stakeholders are kept informed of project progress. There is no guarantee that by using the tool your project will never fall foul of office intrigue and manipulation, but at least by using it you improve your project communication and personalise it. Basically you are trying to pre-empt opposition, assess the risks such opposition brings and reduce those risks.

A US East Coast bank was working on a new internet banking product. The project team had been in place for three months and a reasonable amount of funds had been invested in the project to date. During a project conference call, facilitated by Patrick, one of the participants stated that the project would have to be 'canned'. All the other team members asked why, and the participant answered cryptically, 'I suggest you check my title in the corporate phone directory!' He was VP Internet Security, but this was the first time he had been invited into a project meeting. If the project manager and team had looked into who had the influence and power over all things internet-related they would have saved themselves months of work or at least got one of the key players on board at the very beginning in order to save the project. It was never fully understood whether his objectives were truly technical or personal, but in any case the project stayed canned.

4 WORKPLAN AND TIMINGS *Critical path*

One of the few tools and techniques that is essential to a project manager looking to shorten or 'crunch' the project plan is critical path analysis. However, although it is often mentioned, it is not always completely understood. Many managers understand how to create the critical path within a project but do not fully realise the benefits of this technique and what it can do for them.

In the planning phase of a project, not all activities can, or need, to start at the same time to meet the project's planned completion date. Some activities will be critical to completing the project on time; if they slip by a week then the whole project will slip by a week. Project planners and managers use critical path analysis to identify these activities.

What is the critical path and how do I calculate it?

The critical path is the path through the network of tasks that shows the minimum time needed to finish the project. Software makes life a lot easier for calculations, but understanding the basics to calculate the critical path can really help a project manager and key stakeholders. A few basic techniques will enable you to calculate manually and understand the critical path and its value to you and the project. (See also page 191 in the Director's Toolkit.)

1 **Complete a list of all the activities required to complete the project.** Look at how they interrelate.

2 **Decide which activities have to start immediately or first, which next, and then work through all the tasks until the end of the list.**

3 **Because some activities can happen in parallel, create a network diagram.** This diagram shows the relationship between activities and their dependencies. The diagram can be simple or complex, according to how many activities there are and the number of 'paths' through the project. If you are new to network diagrams, do not underestimate the power of the Post-it note in

planning. Write an activity on each Post-it note, and then, using a flat surface, lay all the Post-its out in a logical sequence or order, remembering that some tasks can be done in parallel. It might look something like the diagram below. This shows a project plan for deciding on, designing and delivering a training course. The critical path is marked in red.

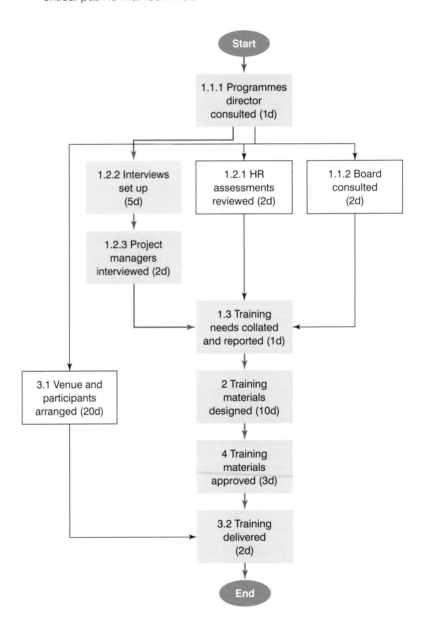

4 Indicate durations of each task and add up the total time required to complete each route ('path') through the network. The longest route is known as the critical path, which shows the shortest possible duration for the project.

So what? What does the critical path do for me?

Once you know the critical path you can understand many other elements of planning your project and the resources required. You can:

→ calculate the start and end dates of the project (add the start date to the critical path total duration and you have a finish date; or, if you prefer, take the project deadline and subtract the total duration of the critical path to create the start date – usually this is the point at which you find out you should have started a week ago);

→ use the network diagram to find opportunities for shortening the project schedule by looking at where you can cut task times on activities on the critical path;

→ use resources wisely by understanding that tasks not on the critical path have some 'slack time' and that allocating resources to these tasks to reduce the overall project duration will not work;

→ understand the progress of the project by closely monitoring the tasks on the critical path, since delays in these tasks will delay the whole project;

→ schedule non-critical path tasks and delay or advance them according to progress;

→ tailor your project diary to ensure that you are supervising the tasks on the critical path as a priority, as opposed to spending time on tasks of less importance.

We are constantly amazed as to why intelligent senior managers seem to think that throwing resources at a project will result in a quicker result. Time after time resources, blood, sweat and tears are spent on tasks that are not on the critical path. Yet management still believe that speeding up those individual tasks will benefit the whole project. A simple explanation of the critical path and how it works and an understanding of the concept of slack time are often all that is needed for senior managers to take a more considered view of allocating resources to speed up projects.

5 ISSUES AND RISKS
Planning contingencies

Well-constructed plans all have at least one thing in common – they all come up against unexpected and changing circumstances. Just because you have activities scheduled in, it doesn't mean they will go according to plan. As a result, good project managers should apply some basic risk management principles to their project and plans.

However, it is not possible to pre-empt every eventuality that could harm the project. It is, therefore, good practice to get the core project team to consider what it will do if certain threats become reality so as to minimise the impact of them. This is, in essence, contingency planning. There are many very complex risk management tools and techniques that can be employed by the project manager today. However, just understanding the basics can really help.

Contingency action plans are there to address the effects of a risk once it has become reality. They are not there to minimise the chance or probability of something happening, but to reduce the effects. You may never use them, but there is a risk you may have to, so plan them in advance. It's as simple as making a decision about an umbrella. You need to take an umbrella with you when going for a walk in case it rains. It's no use when getting wet wishing you had picked up your umbrella on the way out. On the other hand, you may never need the umbrella, so having it may seem an unnecessary burden or expense.

How do I create a contingency plan?

Contingency plans should be part of a full risk management approach, including assessments of risks and pre-emptive actions. However, as a basic, quick tool, try the following process:

1   Discuss the threats to the project plan regularly with the core team and prioritise and decide which threats need the most attention.

2   Be specific and focus upon the top few risks and think through, perhaps with subject matter experts, the possible effects of a risk if it occurs.

3   Create a formal contingency plan and cost it up with whoever supplies the necessary resources.

4   Set a formal 'trigger' with those in charge of the contingency plan. The trigger is an action, event or date whereby the contingency plan is put into action. All involved should know what this trigger is, as without it the contingency plan is useless and has become a waste of resources.

5   Document the contingency plan and triggers and keep them with the project documentation. This information will feed into the next project you do and help in planning future risk management strategies. The plan and triggers should be part of your risk register.

QUICK TIP *FEASIBILITY*

Check feasibility: make sure you are not undertaking a task that cannot be achieved. Review objectives widely beforehand.

Remember that the more stakeholders involved in planning for contingencies, the better the plan. If there is a very strong likelihood that the contingency plan will need to be put into action, then factor it into the project plan in advance so that it becomes part of the plan. Time spent on validating the plan and preparing for problems in advance is rarely time wasted. As a project manager, you should double-check the entire contingency plan before you start to implement the project.

From a personal perspective we have taken contingency planning out of projects and into day-to-day business. Often when travelling around the world to events, conferences and training sessions we are aware that airlines and airports seem to make an increasingly frequent habit of losing luggage. We therefore now take contingency planning to such an extent that we almost expect luggage to be delayed or lost en route. Therefore, when sending materials, handouts, books and so on, we always keep one set of everything with us and all the paperwork on data pens that hang around our necks. If either of us gets to the destination and, surprise surprise, the materials are not there, at least if we can get to a photocopier or a PC and printer we can run off some basic copies to get everything started.

If this, admittedly rather pessimistic, mindset was employed by all project managers, would there be a lot less surprises in projects?

6 THE TEAM *Team selection*

Remember, it is people that make projects successful, not software or systems. So any project manager will want to select the best people for the job and use them effectively. However, many managers feel that they have little leeway when it comes to selecting members of their core project team – they have whom they have and there is very little choice. In addition, many project managers find that they don't have enough people to fill distinctive specialist project roles and that a number of people will have to double up in their roles.

Despite these limitations, it is worth having a look at the techniques that could support you as a project manager in the area of team selection. Build your team carefully, since it will make or break the project. When you have found the person with the right skills, ask yourself:

→ Do I know this person well enough to trust them?

→ Will I be able to work comfortably with them?

→ Will they get along with the other team members?

→ Do they have the skills needed or will they require some training?

Technical skills versus people skills

Think about a very successful project that you have been part of in the past (come on, there must be one!). Then think about the project manager of that successful project and list the skills and abilities of that manager and how they directly contributed to the success of the project. Once you have written them down, divide the skills and abilities into two types – those of a technical nature (e.g. planning skills, content knowledge of the project, risk management skills) and those of an interpersonal nature (e.g. good motivator, good communication skills, empathy, excellent delegation skills). You should find that the effective project manager has a combination of both types of skill – technical and interpersonal.

It is a well-known fact that people tend to recruit in their own image. We recruit those whom we are comfortable with in terms of their attitude and outlook as well as their experience. But therein lies a problem for project managers when creating a core project team. People may have the necessary technical skills for the job but if everyone is technical by nature or training there is a risk that the team may not have much in the way of people skills, or vice versa.

Assess your core team's abilities – are they all technical geniuses but not that comfortable standing up and talking to people and listening to their ideas, or are they the opposite – great empathisers but with little or no content knowledge of the project on hand and no planning skills whatsoever? If this is the case then you need to move towards a balance. Start recruiting to your team people whose skills and, more importantly, abilities complement yours, rather than duplicate them.

Key team roles

In any team you need to look for people to carry out a team role as well as their functional role. To operate efficiently you, as the team leader and project manager, will want someone to perform the following roles:

→ **Coordinator/administrator.** Someone who pulls together the work of the team as a whole and keeps all the paperwork/IT databases up to date.

→ **Critic.** The guardian and analyst of the team's effectiveness, who challenges people when standards and quality drop.

→ **Ideas person.** Someone who innovates and looks for new ways of doing things and for potential shortcuts.

→ **Implementer.** A person who ensures that the team's actions and decisions are put into place and are seen through.

→ **External contact.** Someone who oversees external contacts and relations with third parties.

→ **Inspector.** The quality guru who looks to ensure that a project has high quality throughout and that the team works to high standards. The inspector should always seek to establish new standards and ways of working which raise standards. In contrast to the critic, the inspector should always cite alternatives and options.

→ **Expert.** The technical specialist required for certain parts of the project or for detailed analysis. There may be more than one.

As you appoint people to the team, check off each of these roles to make sure that someone in the team leans towards that sort of contribution. You may discuss this team role with them or not, depending on circumstances (and politics).

Build a team that takes advantage of each individual's skills and avoids the impact of their weaknesses. Remember, especially if you are involved with projects for third parties or external clients, you should ask potential team members if they identify with the aims and objectives of the project. They do not have to agree with them totally but they must at least feel comfortable with why the organisation needs to achieve them.

We are increasingly aware that seniority and job description do not always determine competence, and that when forming a team attitude and dependability count for a lot. In a London-based banking corporation a series of tasks within a major project required the gathering of information from a number of directors and senior managers. They had a reputation for being rather tardy in meeting deadlines that they did not see as being personal priorities. With this in mind, we included in the project team a couple of personal assistants, one of whom especially had a reputation of being something of a Rottweiler when it came to getting jobs done. She took it as an insult on her professional integrity if tasks she asked for were late – irrespective of who the person involved was. Many of the directors and managers involved knew of her and were anxious not to cross her. In terms of getting things done, she was excellent. She was not the most senior member of the team by any means, and she did not have the technical skills for the specific tasks. Yet she had tenacity, and people were concerned about not getting her work done on time. She was the best team member for that part of the project.

7 CRITICAL DECISIONS
Making decisions as a team

Whether in the planning or implementation phase of your project, quality decision making is crucial. New project managers may wish to involve members of the team in making important decisions but this can be fraught with difficulties. Using a decision-making process gets over such problems. Using a formal process may seem over the top at first, and look as though it takes up too much time, but speed will improve with experience. Most importantly, a quality consultative process will help you come to the right decision. The spin-off benefit is that people implement decisions more willingly if they feel that they have been part of the decision-making process.

So, having a logical process is the key to good, team decisions. The only potential drawback, apart from the time issue, is that there is sometimes a risk of 'group-think', where everyone involved comes up with a similar answer or recommendation just when you wanted people to think differently and more widely.

The decision-making process

Here is a simple process for team decision making.

1 **The team must first agree on the criteria against which to measure a decision or course of action**. Ask team members to brainstorm what an ideal solution would look like, using questions such as, 'What benefits should we look for in a solution?'

or 'What should any solution do for us?' This list of criteria can then give you and the team a way of filtering options and comparing the alternatives.

2 **The next stage is to identify which criteria are the most important**. You are looking for the vital criteria against which any alternative option will be judged – the minimum standard.

3 **Now measure all the options available against the ideal agreed for each criterion**. This seems easy but actually requires creativity to evaluate possible decisions effectively.

4 **Continue this measurement and evaluations process until one option stands out**. Encourage debate and discussion at this stage, as you need input from all involved.

5 **Look at this 'final' option – what are the risks around this alternative and how do they weigh against the potential benefits?** If the risks are acceptable and the option meets your decision-making objectives, then go for it. It is your best-balanced decision.

As an example, in the planning phase of a project teams often have to decide which suppliers or contractors to use. Setting clear criteria for how to make those choices will give the team a good start. List these criteria out clearly – for example, 'Will have the necessary number of people on site within a week' or 'Can complete tasks within budget of £20,000'. Understanding which criteria are the most important – cost, speed, quality or a combination of other factors – is critical to helping a team come to a swift decision. Then you can measure the performance of possible suppliers against these criteria to narrow down the available options. Keep discussing the options, refining as you go the criteria and the standards you require against them. This brings you to the best option, and you need quickly to examine the risks that this decision might involve. At the end of the process not only should you have the best decision but also you will have the team's agreement to the decision and their commitment to their role in implementing it.

In many projects, once the decision and choice has been made, the reasons behind it are often lost. In contrast, in a forward-looking learning organisation the criteria for decision making are often kept as a guide for future teams.

You might want an objective critic, who is not part of the core project team, at this stage to review your decision before you implement it – acting as a final 'double-check'. This is important, for as project manager the final responsibility rests with you. Here's a double-checking shortcut that validates the choice using the SAFE acronym:

→ **Suitable.** Is the decision really the most suitable one, given the current state of the project?

→ **Acceptable.** Is the decision acceptable to all the key stake-holders who have an interest in the project – not just those involved in making the decision?

→ **Feasible.** Will the implementation of the decision be practical and feasible, given time, resources and skills available?

→ **Enduring.** Will the solution or course of action decided upon endure to the end of the project and into the long term, or is it just a short-term solution?

QUICK TIP **OBJECTIVES**

Make sure that your objectives are measurable. Use SMART objectives whenever possible (see page 41).

---

8 RESOURCES AND BUDGET
Creating a project budget

When it comes to finances and budgeting, many people – particularly technical project managers – start to worry. It is not their natural ground to cost up a project; but until you create a full project budget there is no way of calculating whether the project will generate a positive return on investment (ROI). It is unlikely that a project will be given authorisation to go ahead without an accurate and detailed idea of costs, yet people seem to think that they can fudge financial planning.

What you need is a basic tool to work out costs for a project – the **resources matrix**.

This is a document showing what resources you will need and how much they will or might cost. This document is also the basis for gaining the commitment of all the stakeholders and managers who will supply the necessary resources. Create a matrix showing all the activities that make up the project, and the resources required, broken down by type, the amount required and the cost. The headings in the matrix should be relevant to your project. Include a 'special' column to record and cost up all resources that are unique or highly costly to your project or may have a long lead time. Costing them up separately is a way of highlighting their value to the project.

Here is a simple example of a section of a small project for the production of marketing materials, highlighting some of the resources and people involved in specific tasks.

TASK	STANDARD CONSUMABLES	EQUIPMENT	GRAPHICS MATERIALS	FACILITIES	SPECIAL	TOTAL
1.1	A0 plotter paper €500/ream 2 reams = €1,000	CAD software licence €4,000			Drafting ink €1,000	€6,000
1.2			Leaflets €20/'000 €2,000	Overflow office rental €5,000		€7,000
1.3					Licence for photos €5,000	€5,000
2.1				Studio hire photo shoot 1 day €8,000		€8,000
Project						€26,000

The same principles can now be applied for the human resources you may be using in the project. Create a **responsibility assignment matrix** (see opposite page) that has across the top all those people who are contributing to the project, chargeable or non-chargeable, depending upon your organisation's costing mechanisms. The difference between the costing of human resources is the use of day rates and the amount of time you need the people in the project plan. You can, of course, combine the two matrices.

TASK	GRAPHIC DESIGNER	PHOTOGRAPHER	ASSISTANT	ART MANAGER	COPYWRITER	TOTAL
1.1	2 days to create first draft of leaflets €1,000/day €2,000			Approve draft and amend €1,200/day 0.5 day = €600	1 day to insert text into graphic leaflet €1,000/day €1,000	€3,600
1.2						
1.3		3-day photo shoot €10,000	3-day photo shoot €6,000	Support for design €1,000		€17,000
2.1	4 days to insert of photos and artwork €2,000			Final approval €1,200		€3,200
Project						€23,800

There may be a good reason to separate the capital costs (one-off expenditure subject to depreciation) from the revenue costs (materials, services and people costs). In either case, the bottom of the matrices should be combined to get a working estimate of the costs of the project. This figure should be added to the project statement and will give any senior management reviewing the project an idea of whether the project is cost effective. It also gives the accountants the opportunity to calculate the return on investment (ROI).

Without a full breakdown of the costs, human and other, it is impossible for stakeholders to assess what the ROI will be. Many companies break down their capital costs, ignoring their staff costs, and although they deliver the project they never get round to comparing the short-term costs of delivering the project against the long-term benefits of the project. Very little project measurement ever gets done afterwards. When we ask companies why this is so, we usually get the answer that people are already busy on the next project and have no time to go back over the results and compare them against the planned costs. Generally these organisations never improve the projects they do – but they still carry on delivering projects, some with real, unmeasured, value and some with none.

If you are not happy with figures, and many managers are not, then always try to check the numbers with a project cost accountant. Use standard costs and figures where available, and check how your company treats overheads as project charges.

9 PROJECT LEADERSHIP *Delegation*

What activities should you delegate within your project and what should you never delegate? Remember the golden rule – you can delegate *authority* to someone else for a part of the project but ultimately the *responsibility* for the delivery of the project always remains with you, the project manager. It is a poor project manager who hides behind their people when, for example, mistakes are made.

There are many tools for managers to use in delegating work to others but the question of what you should delegate can be tricky. From a business perspective you should delegate anything that can be done quicker, better and cheaper by someone else apart from you. However, there are a number of tasks that should not be passed on to others, no matter how competent those people may be. These include:

→ **Praise.** It rather dilutes the effect if you ask others to thank people on your behalf. Always make the effort to thank people personally – either by phone, email or face to face. Asking other people to give out your praise sends quite a contrary message – you value their efforts and hard work but not quite enough to thank them personally.

→ **Reward.** This is an extension of praise in a more material way. Giving rewards is always the preserve of line managers, and this means that within the context of a project it is the preserve of the project manager.

→ **Issues of discipline.** Managing disciplinary matters is not just about managing poor performance or poor quality of work but also about addressing issues that affect the working and results of the project team. As project manager, you should deal with these directly.

→ **Managing the sponsor.** Managing the relationship with the sponsor has to be done by the project manager. You cannot delegate this key management relationship.

→ **Confidentiality.** If people have requested a degree of confidentiality on an issue or your personal guarantee of secrecy, then delegation is clearly not an option – if you wish to retain credibility.

Patrick was once called into an organisation to help get a project back on track and was confronted by a very stressed-out project manager. He was clearly an expert in the project subject but it soon became clear that because he was so expert he felt that no one could do the work as well as he and therefore he did not delegate. Other members of staff also recognised his expertise and a vicious circle ensued where other people did not offer their help as they knew that their knowledge was not at the same level as the expert project manager. The project manager rapidly became the project 'doer'. He got involved in every piece of detail and lost the big picture. He did try to delegate work but either found it difficult to explain what he required or complained that it was just as quick to do it himself.

He was quite right. In the very short term delegation does not save time. However, in the medium to long term, making the effort to explain what is required and to what level will save time. The danger is that as the project falls behind schedule the project manager feels they have even less time to delegate work, and so on and so on.

Delegating effectively

Delegation is all about the distribution of work or management to make things more effective or efficient. It is therefore crucial to delegate tasks in a way that minimises the chance of confusion or miscommunication. Your project management approach must seek to clarify tasks, outline objectives and improve communication. By doing this, and focusing upon making all tasks clear and measurable, you will make the task of delegation easier. With practice, delegation becomes natural and you may even get a reputation as a project manager that allows your staff the freedom to act independently within the project. This has great benefits when trying to attract the best people in your organisation to your projects. They know they are going to be trusted to get on with it and that they are going to learn and develop.

It can be useful to subdivide a project into a number of sub-projects as well as tasks. A sub-project is a discrete piece of work within a project, which when combined with the other tasks completes the whole project. Identifying sub-projects can be a powerful medium for delegation, giving responsibility to another team member for a discrete sub-objective of the project.

As well as making sure that the tasks you have delegated are SMART (see page 41), a simple checklist will help to ensure that you are on the right track:

1 **Check that the task is suitable for delegation in the first place**. Make sure it is not one of the tasks that is essential for you to do. In a project environment, most tasks are delegated for reasons of resource efficiency and/or technical ability. You need someone to do something because of your lack of time and/or skills.

2 **Make sure that the individuals or teams who you have in mind have the necessary skills, abilities, attitude and time to do what you ask**. In a project environment, as opposed to 'business as usual', you will not have time to train or develop others to make them suitable for some tasks that you would like to delegate. This is a test of the skills sets that have been part of your selection criteria when choosing project team members.

3 **Part of the 'contract' in delegating work is an explanation of what is being delegated and why**. The 'why' should include an element of 'why them?' and 'what's in it for them?'. Make sure you explain how the tasks fit in with the project objectives.

4 **Clearly state the desired results**. This means setting quality standards, timescales, deadlines and your definition of success.

The clearer this is, the greater the chance of success, first time. Make sure review dates, times and deadlines are very clear, understood and agreed.

5 **As part of defining the desired results, there should be some discussion of the resources available for the task at hand**. There may be some leeway for change at this stage, but often resources have already been agreed and there may be very little room for manoeuvre. Make that clear as well, to avoid the person delegated coming to you for more resources as they carry out the task.

6 **Give ongoing support**. While avoiding the temptation to interfere is crucial, it is necessary for you, the project manager, to ensure that the person or persons you have delegated to know how and when they can access you for any reason. Agreeing a means by which you can monitor progress will also avoid the charge of interfering during the task period. Remember, you are delegating not abdicating.

7 **Review performance**. Ideally, as soon as the delegated tasks have been completed the project manager should review performance with those people delegated to do the task. However, in reality, this is often left until the end of the project or phase. The key is that it should be done, and as soon as practicable.

Delegation does not have to be limited to physical tasks. The delegation of the management of tasks or parts of the project is where experienced project managers free up more time. This comes with experience, but using tools like the resources matrix and the responsibility assignment matrix will make the delegation of management easier.

Delegation isn't the only skill required of project managers and leaders – they also need to be able to inspire, motivate and take a high-level view. But without delegation, less time will be available to focus on these other skills.

10 COMMUNICATIONS
Communication plan

For a project to run smoothly, the resources required must be available at the time you need them. This demands planning – of people, facilities, equipment and resources. A complete project plan guides the project and is the document that communicates everything from your overall objectives, through activities, to resources required and schedules. It includes the master schedule, Gantt chart, objectives and other key documents crucial to the successful delivery of the project within budget, deadlines and targets. Think of the communication plan as being a sub-set of the project plan.

It is important to make information available to the people who need it, when they need it and in the right format. Your challenge as a project manager is to facilitate and encourage this communication within and outside the project team. Ensure that all project data is up to date and recorded efficiently – this will then allow you to disseminate information as required. The ideal is to have a project management office (PMO) for managing multiple projects, but on a smaller scale a knowledge centre is equally valuable – often known as the 'war room'.

The knowledge centre

Remember that each item of project information has some potential value to someone. In most cases it will be obvious what needs to be stored, but try to think more widely and take a longer view. Could this seemingly trivial piece of information be of value to another project manager after this project has finished? In this age of high-speed information technology and bandwidth, there is no reason not to store something due to lack of capacity.

Appoint a coordinator to be in charge of managing all the information. They should be responsible for getting the data in from team members and giving out the right data at the right time in the right format to the stakeholders. This data could be, for example, Gantt charts, activity reports, risk registers or issue logs. Many a time we have been part of a project meeting where everyone gets out their own copy of the project Gantt chart and after about five minutes of comparing copies it becomes clear that we are not all singing from the same hymn sheet. A good project administrator is usually the sole person in charge of the version control process, and in well-managed projects this administrator will issue the latest, common, up-to-date version of the Gantt chart for all to see.

There is also a risk that the project team gets swamped with data, so think about the following in advance.

1 **What data do I require to manage the project and how shall I classify it?** Try classifying information by dividing data into the following categories:
   → General planning information: objectives, vision statement, master schedule, network diagrams.
   → General data: background information that might be useful to carry out activities.
   → Completed activities: data gathered on finished tasks.
   → Activities in progress: data required for people carrying out activities now.
   → Activities not yet started: data that might be useful for up and coming tasks and activities.

2 **Who needs what data, when and in what format?** Apart from the members of the project team, who should have access to the knowledge centre? There are also probably others outside the organisation who could benefit from information you can share.
   → Refer to the list of stakeholders you made at the start of the project as part of the stakeholder analysis.
   → Categorise those who are crucial to the project and therefore will get data as a priority.
   → Plan how you are going to make the data available. It could be 'push' – i.e. sending data out to them, which requires your active management at specific times – or 'pull' – i.e. posting data somewhere for them to find. The rule should be that this takes as little time as possible for you or your knowledge coordinator to manage.
   → Review the format of the data, the timings and the content with the stakeholders and team members.

Knowledge and information are the oil that keeps the project running smoothly, but in general people do not appreciate this until they feel 'out of the loop'.

STOP - THINK - ACT

This chapter has included a variety of tools and techniques used by the world's most successful companies to optimise their performance in the area of project management. Some will be more relevant than others to you, and some may need to be adapted to suit your specific situation. Most project managers will use these tools at some point in their career, though maybe not all at once. Take time now to reflect on the top ten project management tools and techniques, and identify elements that you will include in your project management.

What should we do?	What tools and techniques are appropriate?
Who do we need to involve?	Who needs to be involved and why?
What resources will we require?	What information, facilities, materials, equipment or budget will be required?
What is the timing?	How long will each activity typically take?

Visit **www.Fast-Track-Me.com** to use the Fast Track online planning tool.

Contemporary project management and leadership

Professor Svein Arne Jessen

For many years projects were seen as single operations following strict rules of specification, time and budget, but this view is being overtaken by the notion that projects are the means for much more comprehensive change which involves many more unknowns. Many organisations have now grouped projects with their own specific goals into programmes with broadly common objectives. In this way companies have moved up a gear and started to 'manage by projects', in order to deliver higher-order strategic objectives, which would not be possible if the projects were treated independently. Further, as the number of projects and project programmes within companies grows, the emphasis shifts to the management of the total 'portfolio of projects', implying that as strategic imperatives change new projects may be created and earlier ones terminated, regardless of individual project viability against its initial objectives. In consequence project managers now need to pay attention to three dimensions: thinking 'inwards' on how to be successful with their single project; thinking 'upwards' on the strategic fit for their project; and thinking 'sideways' on how their single project may be combined with other projects to form a better project portfolio.

A widening of the scope of projects, and, at the same time, the use of the project concept for a broadening range of activities (including both physical projects and 'soft areas' such as organisational change), has led to a shift in thinking about the role of projects in a modern society. There is an increasing recognition that projects act as 'influencing agents' instead of being a reaction to societal trends. This has led to three particular concerns for organisations:

1 The extent to which the projects' base organisation is mature enough to handle a range of highly complex projects, so that it can provide adequate support.

2 The existence of a strong belief in the benefits of using projects for implementing change.

3 The degree to which there is a climate among its stakeholder group for active knowledge-building relating to the impact of projects.

Project maturity within the business community is the sum of the ability to act and a willingness to be involved, and an understanding of the impact of project willingness and project action. Understanding, knowledge, learning and acting are closely related and will play an active and interactive role in building a desired attitude for change through projects. The division of labour and the rationality of the decision process, together with good lines of communication and a well understood and accepted authority structure, enhance the operational capability. Projects will be best managed when they have a mix of 'cultural' and 'structural' elements embodied in the project process. The principle that risk has to be treated differently depending on the level within the organisation seems, then, to be valid for projects in general. At lower levels, risks are within the control of the key project actors and should be handled by them, while risks at higher levels can only be handled appropriately through an understanding of projects in relation to both the strategy of the company or the organisation and, at the same time, the external environment seen from a wider angle. That projects should be

EXPERT VOICE

part of a hierarchy within an organisation in order to be handled professionally is a very important message today, just as at the individual level major operations can only be understood when put into a strategic framework.

A second concern is how, then, to measure real project success. Traditionally project success was viewed narrowly as the achievement of intended outcomes in terms of specification, time and budget. While this was widely accepted in early notions of project management, when the project context shifted it became apparent that a broader set of outcome measures was needed. Such influences include the growing concern to ensure maximisation of the lifetime value of the project endeavour, the notion of the sustainable enterprise, the importance of knowledge as the source of competitive advantage, and the importance of motivation as a source for better project execution. Within knowledge-based enterprises, projects are today being considered as important arenas for learning; the uniqueness of each project makes project work rich in personal and organisational learning opportunities. So, in modern projects, success is a broad concept that deals with the impact of the project overall, i.e. both project management success and project end-product success. Expanding the success criteria in this way will necessarily postpone the final judgement of the project – often months or years after the completion of the project itself – to include lifetime performance measures. Given this broader set of expected outcomes it is obvious that project management needs to respond rather differently than before. Both policy makers and project managers can benefit from understanding the interrelationship of factors that need particular attention, in order to achieve these outcomes and the eventual establishment of new performance indicators for the management of projects.

The third area of particular concern has to do with the way projects are executed. There has long been recognition that ICT has influenced our way of thinking and behaving. Technology has not only relieved us of much boring, repetitive work, enabling us to focus our attention on more advanced, innovative and creative thinking, but it has also made us able to do things faster and more comprehensively than ever before. For projects, this development has had a strong influence on project execution and control, replacing the old notion that operations can be undertaken in a logical series of steps. Decision making based on a time-consuming and linear process of data collection, analysis, elaboration, then conclusions and then perhaps publication and action has been significantly compressed and rapid decision processes made possible. The 'scrum' concept has emerged for project execution. Borrowed from baseball and later refined using the 'action research and action learning' principle, it recommends stand-up-meetings on an every-morning basis, in sequences of three to four weeks, where project teams are invited to bring in new developments and thoughts, and change the project process where appropriate. Project control is norm-nally closely related to the project plan, hence the measures adopted fail to take into account the extent the project processes are using the latest developments in the field.

EXPERT VOICE

TECHNOLOGIES

To remain as effective and efficient as possible, Fast Track managers differentiate themselves by the support mechanisms they put in place to help themselves and their team. These include the intelligent use of appropriate technologies – enabling, for example, the automation of non-core activities, thereby freeing up time to focus on managing, motivating and leading people. They may also include the use of coaches, peer-to-peer networks, and gaining access to the latest thinking in the field. However, information technology, especially in the sphere of project and programme management, can, if badly managed, often get in the way of effective management rather than support it.

Getting started

Why consider technology?

Technology at its best can be an enabler. It can help the project manager cope with the rapid rate of change in the external environment by keeping them abreast of changes in the relevant sector or business. In a complex business and within a multifunctional project, how can a project manager possibly hope to keep up to date and remain aware of what is going on?

There is certainly no shortage of information channels, from social networking sites and blogs to specialist forums and special interest groups – frankly, there is too much. How do project managers sift through the myriad of emails, websites, reports, conference calls and mobile texts that arrive at all times of the day and night?

While information overload is a critical issue, the reality is that if we don't make use of relevant and up-to-date information then we will fall behind the competition. While technology is not the answer to all our problems, it is a very important enabler to help us remain effective and efficient – especially within project management.

QUICK TIP **SCHEDULING**
Remember to keep your plans up to date at all times, and have a date or version number on them if you print them out.

How do I free up time?

Before deciding how to use automation/technology to save time, first you need to eliminate entirely low-value or unnecessary activities.

Make a list of everything you do on a week-to-week basis. Assess how much time is spent on each, as well as the value you associate with each – perhaps using a simple five-point scale. Then draw a simple two by two matrix to assess where each activity falls:

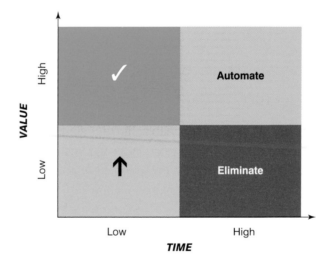

→ Those falling in the bottom right-hand corner are the critical ones to address – high time but low value. Eliminate these. For example, perhaps there are meetings you don't need to attend or some that could be delegated to a member of your team, which might also be good for their personal development.

→ Those in the bottom left-hand corner pose a problem. They are not consuming much time, so are reasonably efficient, but they are not delivering a lot of value. Perhaps there is a way of improving the value of each activity. You might, for example, change the agenda on a weekly operational update meeting to include asking the team to come up with at least one new idea for improvement. Many personal administration issues are in this quadrant – such as how you file your project-related emails and document the filing system for all project reports. They add little value to the project and if dealt with straight away take little time; however, if you leave the filing and sorting of reports to build up, they will consume a disproportionate amount of time.

→ Activities in the top left-hand box are already efficient and of high value. Perhaps they are already automated, so leave them until your next review. These could include, for example, the communication of tasks and updating jobs. If you have a communications process in hand then this will be automatic, but without it the project simply cannot go ahead.

→ In the top right-hand box are activities such as the origination and initial thinking and planning of projects. It can take a lot of time to initiate projects in the right manner, so these activities are by definition important – high value. Although you do not want to get rid of these activities, you do need to find a more efficient way of doing them. For example, it may be that the monthly meeting you have with a regional distributor could be managed using video conferencing.

Think carefully about your overall time management: be aware of how you use your time and constantly look to find ways of improving this.

Once you have conducted a time–value assessment, you will be more conscious of this need. Don't forget that we tend to do those things that we enjoy and put off what is less fun. If you're serious about putting technology to the best possible use then try to overcome this psychological bias and look at the use of your time as objectively as you can. If you do not manage your time well, you will find it difficult to manage the project in addition to your other job-related activities.

When invited to meetings, constantly ask the question 'Why?' What value will the meeting give you, or what value will you give to it? If there is no obvious answer, then decline the invitation or delegate. Try a more targeted agenda or do more preparation before the meeting to reduce the meeting duration itself. The key is to remove unnecessary tasks and activities before looking for opportunities to automate: that way you avoid putting IT and other resources into something that has little or no value.

Finally, encourage your team to carry out the same exercise so that when you are deciding on various options for automation you are aiming to increase the overall effectiveness of the team, not just yourself.

The process-system link

How should we use technology?

Think carefully about how you will use technology and ensure it links back to what you are seeking to achieve. Perhaps the starting point is to look at your overall project management framework for opportunities to make each element quicker, simpler and possibly more fun. It could be that the technology might aid reporting, or planning, or even implementation. In our opinion, it is very rare that technology helps with all three. Facilitation of learning, however, can be greatly enhanced through IT. Anything that aids in the learning process – before, during and after a project – must be worthwhile.

Some aspects of the framework will lend themselves to the use of technologies, whereas some of the softer areas, such as leadership and culture, will offer fewer opportunities or, if poorly applied, may even weaken your position as project manager.

You can also choose to use all kinds of project management software, ranging in sophistication from the simple use of Microsoft Excel to produce Gantt charts through to automated, enterprise-wide solutions such as Primavera.

 CASE STORY **SURREY BORDERS PARTNERSHIP NHS (FOUNDATION) TRUST, FIONA'S STORY**

Narrator Fiona is the CEO of the merged entity of three NHS Trusts and required up-to-date reporting of this large project portfolio of merger activities.

Context Following NHS reorganisation, three mental health Trusts in the Surrey area were required to merge into a single entity. The Audit Commission had identified a best practice approach to the merger and integration, and core projects had been identified and linked to Audit Commission objectives.

Issue The Trust management had been through PRINCE2 training and found it overcomplicated. The senior management team of the three Trusts were facing a round of redundancies and skill levels in project management were acknowledged as being low.

Solution A web-based tool gave Fiona immediate access to status reports for all projects across all three Trusts. She used a Red, Amber, Green (RAG) status indicator to flag up areas of concern and focus senior management's time on key projects. Project managers were required to update information on a bi-weekly basis as a minimum.

Learning By using a live tool in review meetings, the amount of time spent in creating paper-based reports was minimised and over 20 per cent of administration time was saved. In addition, key decisions were highlighted and made visible to all senior managers. The three Trusts had over 200 sites so a web-based tool ensured that all could input data, irrespective of location.

Top technologies

How do I know what technology exists?

So we now understand the need for technology, systems and automation and where we are going to deploy it for best effect, but how do we find out what is available?

Get into the habit of scanning for technology trends on the web or in industry journals. Look at what other people in your business are reading – particularly those you most admire. Where do they get their information? The web can easily be a distraction, so be wary of getting carried away with your research and straying into 'surfing' rather than specific research.

However, be aware that there is a lot of information available, and there are new technologies coming along all the time. How do you decide what is relevant and what is useful? Start with a healthy scepticism. Investigate the technology, but ask the 'So what?' question – is this relevant to my team and to me, and how will it impact performance? Look at available project management software, which covers many types of activity such as scheduling, cost control and budget management, resource allocation, collaboration, communication, quality management and documentation or administration systems. Choose wisely – use the V-SAFE criteria as a test: does the technology add **value**, is it **suitable**, **acceptable** and **feasible**, and will it give **enduring** benefits? Does it provide value for money and does it link to other systems currently in place? Check those criteria before making a Go/No Go/Wait decision.

 QUICK TIP **RESOURCE PLANNING**
Refine your resources matrix until anyone could work from it. Simple is better.

What tools will support a sustainable approach to project management?

Recognise that the development of technologies is moving so quickly that the list of what is available to you will never be static. Use the following list as a challenge to what is possible, but remember that it is a snapshot of what is happening at a point in time. The key is to get into the habit of constantly scanning this field in search of ideas for improving the effectiveness and efficiency of your project management framework.

1 Project management and the internet

What is it?

What would we do without the internet? The internet has a myriad of sites where 'Gantt heads' (those into project management on the internet) can go for free downloads, support or forums. It is an excellent tool. However, like a library where the covers from all the books have been removed, it may take some time to find what you want and what is useful. Professional bodies in the area of project management, such as the Association of Project Managers (APM) and the Project Management Institute (PMI), are excellent portals where you can go for advice, get in contact with others and find links to third-party sites.

Pros

It provides a rich source of information on a variety of project-related topics. The information is often free and you can get hold of it very fast. The internet can provide a wealth of information about tools, software, systems and case studies in a matter of minutes where previously it would have taken weeks. It also encourages creativity, as noted by US journalist Franklin P. Adams: 'I find that a great part of the information I have was acquired by looking up something and finding something else on the way.'

Cons

Most of the information contains a degree of bias. After all, someone has produced it for their own purposes. It is also typically unstructured, in that a search on a topic will yield lots of results but the information on each site will be laid out in a different style. Some people call it a repository of several trillion words (and growing); the trouble is locating the 25 words you really need.

Success factors

Beware of information overload, and if new information is of critical importance then validate the information before drawing your conclusions using other sources. A neat rule of thumb is the one that journalists use – only publish a 'fact' if you have got at least two reliable sources. There are many useful sites but the best practitioners of all things 'internet' create their own collection of 'favourites'. Create a list of sites that have something specific for you to use. Subdivide them into categories, such as software, forums, research, project management methods, case studies, professional bodies (i.e. APM, PMI), etc.

QUICK TIP **WORK BREAKDOWN STRUCTURE**

When creating a work breakdown structure (WBS) include a verb and put it in the past tense. For example, 'materials ordered' or 'manual written'. This is because a WBS needs to show action, as this will help with resource and time planning.

2 Spreadsheet software

What is it?

The most basic of office tools can have a dramatic effect on the management of projects. Commonly purchased products that help in many other areas of business can have specific relevance to project management. In particular, the spreadsheet, although designed for managing numbers, can help the project manager in many ways, such as planning tasks in the work breakdown structure (WBS).

Pros

Most organisations have spreadsheet software installed in their businesses. They are excellent for the creation of basic Gantt charts; in fact a simple spreadsheet is many new project managers' first experience of Gantt charts and their creation. Spreadsheets are also very useful for creating a WBS – essentially a list of tasks to do, subdivided into their constituent parts.

Cons

The spreadsheet is not specifically built for project management and therefore is somewhat limited in its scope. In our experience, as soon as a project manager starts to try to manage two or more projects, competing for the same resources, on a single spreadsheet application, the complexity increases. Spreadsheets are often referred to as 'flat files' (i.e. it not a database), which means that they are fine for single projects but not so useful when you have multiple projects and want to share and extract data between them – making modifications to the spreadsheet then becomes time consuming and difficult.

Success factors

In a frequently changing project it becomes a real chore to have to 'cut and paste' new tasks into a spreadsheet; or, if members change the format of the spreadsheet to adapt to their specific needs, then merging them back together into a master task list becomes near impossible. The success factor is therefore simplicity. Remember that the more complex your project and project management environment, the more complex your needs. The more projects you manage and the greater the need to share information between them, the more likely it is that a simple spreadsheet will not meet your requirements and you will rapidly cross over from being aided by software to being restricted by it.

3 Word-processing applications

What are they?

These are probably the most common and widespread of applications – even though they may not seem like project management tools. The most effective project managers are those who harness common technologies, such as Microsoft Word, and make them work for them. Turning out project-specific templates using Word can quickly save you time.

Pros	If the overall need is to communicate such things as project charters and/or objectives then a word-processing application is perfect for your needs. With a little more effort, templates can be created and before you know it you have a 'home grown' methodology driving your projects. A template will force a certain method and go some way to ensuring a certain standard of compliance.
Cons	While useful in communicating objectives and concepts, word-processing applications do little in the planning and implementation stages of project management. That's not to say that a project manager will not find such applications valuable, but they are not specialist in nature and have limited usefulness in certain areas of project management.
Success factors	Use word-processing applications to communicate with team members about objectives and basic timelines, in order to build more effective teams. Try to create templates and forms that can be reused on subsequent projects. These will not only save you time but will also start to create a standard to which others can work.

4 Project management software

What is it?	Project management software applications (such as Microsoft Project, Primavera, WBS Tracker, etc.) are used to scope, plan, monitor and control the implementation of projects using recognised project management techniques. They provide a structured approach to managing complex projects and are fit-for-purpose in that they are designed for project management.
Pros	Project management software provides a very effective way of planning project activities, communicating objectives, allocating tasks, scheduling activities and resources, and monitoring progress. Simple outputs can also provide clear reports for all stakeholders. Web-based applications used across an organisation also provide a means for managing the portfolio of projects as a whole, as opposed to managing individual projects in isolation. Generally IT departments are happy to give permission to use web-based tools, as they are easy to manage and require no downloads or physical inputs to their systems.
Cons	Most project management tools are too complex for the simpler projects. In addition, some of the most popular and well-known project tools are so over-engineered as to make them virtually unusable for all but the most specialist and professionally qualified of project managers. They tend to focus on detailed task and resource management as opposed to the typical success factors, such as having clear objectives, an effective stakeholder management process and a simple risk register. Some applications can be prohibitively

expensive and IT departments generally dislike having to install and support specialist software.

Success factors

Even with all-encompassing project management software, there are risks to the novice project manager. A good starting point is to understand your needs as a project manager and the requirements of those around you. Look for a simple and easy-to-use web-based software product that meets your specific needs. Then ensure that you and key stakeholders know how to use it. For example, if your need is for project reporting, then find a tool that does that for you; if your requirement is for resource planning and scheduling, then find a tool that does that instead. Finally, don't forget that project management is as much about setting the vision and leading the team as producing impressive, if esoteric, charts and diagrams.

Example

This web-based report below shows all the projects within the Benelux region. A simple Red-Amber-Green classification is used to identify projects needing attention. During a review meeting, the team will 'drill down' into the detail of projects needing support.

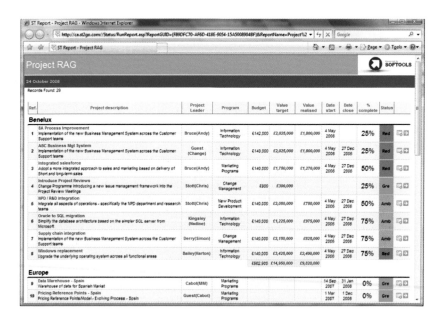

5 Video conferencing

What is it?

Video conferencing allows people to communicate with both voice and video even if the other person is located elsewhere in the world – rather like having a telephone conversation with someone and being able to see them at the same time. This technology has been around for a long time, but with increased internet speeds and improved flat-screen displays, it is getting cheaper and better all the time. The ability to show documents to the other people in the call is a very useful feature and can be effectively used in planning schedules and Gantt charts on multisite projects worldwide.

Pros

The obvious advantage is that it cuts down on travel, thereby reducing costs and freeing up your time. This will have the greatest impact on companies that have high levels of spending on international flights, but it also has the potential to dramatically reduce domestic travel costs. Some systems will also tell you when the other person is available, and personal desktop-based systems are convenient and very easy to use.

Cons

Setting up video conferencing facilities within a company can be expensive, and many systems just do not offer the quality required for effective communications. They are often very impersonal, and so even when the quality of the signal is good, it does not provide personal contact and can be ineffective in, for example, sales situations.

Success factors

Investigate internet-based technologies and consider using a standard version in a pilot situation, i.e. within a small team, in order to work out whether this technology is appropriate and, if so, how you want to use it. You will need to establish management routines in terms of what to use and when to make it effective. However, in our experience, video conferencing is still a poor substitute for a face-to-face meeting at a crucial part of a project. A project kick-off meeting, for instance, is a chance to motivate and inspire which can't really be done over a phone line.

6 Email

What is it?

Electronic mail allows members of a project team to communicate via their computers. This has become the standard form of communication across and within businesses and is a key tool for effective communications.

Pros

Most organisations already have email systems, with many being free of charge. Furthermore, even though the systems are complex, most people have such a high level of familiarity that they are comfortable using them. (When email was first released the CEO of one of the top FTSE 100 companies said that it would never take off!) Email systems have also become an ersatz filing system for keeping messages and reports and as such many project managers have an email filing system specifically designed for their projects.

Cons	Unfortunately, most email systems are open to a certain amount of abuse, and suffer from two issues. First, there may be a tendency to copy people in unnecessarily to keep them informed – becoming internal junk mail. Alternatively, it is easy to communicate one-on-one without including other key stakeholders in the discussion. In addition, email can stifle personal interaction: while working in a software company in the 1990s Simon found it odd that programmers and developers, working on the same project, would do *all* their communication via email and even have debates about detailed issues online – while all seated in the same room! Remember, too, that communications between members of the team often contain useful insights and lessons learned, but unless you take action to file emails, these tend to get lost on completion of the project.
Success factors	Use email selectively to direct members of the team and to communicate with key stakeholders. Set up distribution lists for certain members of the project team or stake-holders to make communication in projects simpler. However, use alternative tools for managing the projects, and specifically for capturing the vital lessons learned. Success is in realising that email is for communication – and little else.

7 Blogs and forums

What are they?	These are special websites that allow people to log in and discuss ideas relating to a specific topic in the form of a discussion thread, where the most recent comments are displayed first. Blogs may be created on the internet or on the company intranet and provide a place where groups of people that work together can share ideas. These groups are now often known as communities of practice (CoPs).
Pros	They provide a more open form of discussion than emails, as the discussion is open for others to see and is captured for future reference by other teams. Blogs work particularly well where they are focused on a specific topic – sometimes referred to as special interest groups (SIGs).
Cons	Unless there is a clear reason for going to the blog, many people just don't bother, so a team leader has to encourage a team to use it and build it into their normal processes. Blogs often work best for IT teams, where they already have a culture of sharing insights and expertise, but may not work so well with other teams or departments.
Success factors	Consider carefully whether you would use a blog, and if so how? What would make it exciting and worthwhile enough to make it work within the project management community, when most people will have other commitments

to focus on? Perhaps find a small team that would be interested in piloting a blog on a specific topic and see how they get on. Think about rolling out successful blogs within the organisation to a wider audience – blogs seem to gain a momentum of their own for the most trivial of reasons. This might increase the interest in projects and project management generally within the organisation.

8 Digital dashboard

What is it?   A digital dashboard is a term that refers to the presentation of performance data on a computer screen – whether the manager's PC or via an LCD projector in a meeting. The senior member of the project board defines the information displayed on a project dashboard.

Pros   If set up correctly they provide an instant update on progress every time a member of the team logs in to their PC – 'pushing' relevant data directly to the person with the greatest level of interest or need. For example, we set up a project management reporting system in an NHS Trust. As well as managing the project meetings, a 20 per cent saving in administration time was generated through the use of online real-time reports, not to mention the amount of paper saved. Some dashboards can report data in real time – that is, live information fed in is instantly available for display and does not have to wait to be processed as a 'report.'

Cons   They can be costly to set up, as the underlying data typically needs to be pulled from other databases and put into a format that makes it presentable. Too often the data is not relevant to the individual user and may not be up to date. Digital dashboards can also radically change the culture of an organisation that is used to lengthy meetings and having plenty of time to prepare reports. Such radical change can be upsetting for some managers.

Success factors   Investigate the pros and cons of creating a project dashboard for your business – what would it look like, what information would you want it to present and how would it support your project management framework? Once set up, make sure that it reflects the different needs of the different stakeholders that will be using it. If meetings are problematic, then these tools can be very helpful and the benefits across the business in reducing administration can be immense.

9 Lessons-learned database

What is it?   A central repository of the lessons learned from previous project initiatives. It captures basic information about the project, the management, decisions made, the risks and the teams involved. It will ideally also present a 'story' of what was done and why, what the outcome was (good or bad) and perhaps what the team would do differently next time. It could even be linked into project review meetings.

Pros

It is enormously valuable to the business as a means of capturing insights from individuals and teams while they remember and before they move on to new projects or jobs – or worse still leave the business. Without active use of a lessons-learned database, organisations often repeat mistakes in terms of selecting bad ideas or implementing new ideas badly. The database should inform the next project you get involved with and colour your judgement appropriately. In fact, in one major pharmaceutical firm we work with it is standard operating procedure (SOP) for project managers to review the 'project lessons-learned database' before starting a new project, looking for tips, techniques and similar projects.

Cons

Teams often don't invest the time to stop, think and learn, let alone capture the ideas for future reuse by others. Towards the end of the project many members of the team will have moved on to other commitments and they often just don't have the time. Even when insights are captured, people often don't believe that others will bother to look at them, so they are often unstructured and of little value.

Success factors

Make capturing of insights part of weekly review meetings with the team, and ensure they are captured and classified in a central, easily accessible database. Don't wait to the end of the project to do this or it will never be done. To bring the database to life, make sure that future teams are encouraged to review the database during the initial idea evaluation and project planning phases. Project directors and sponsors should, in our opinion, prevent formal closure of projects until the lessons-learned database has been completed.

QUICK TIP PEOPLE

Draw up a list of people and their specific skills, who you think may be able to help you on future projects.

How do I keep balance?

Now stop. Before going out and investing in the latest and greatest, remember that technology is just an enabler. Success will ultimately depend on your ability to lead others, your behaviours and how you interact with others.

Be wary of being drawn into new technologies too quickly – let some-one else make the mistakes, but then learn quickly. Finally, if you do decide to introduce new systems to your team, think carefully about the possible risks – what could go wrong?

STOP – THINK – ACT

You may already have been aware of many of these modern technologies, but you should now understand how each can be used to support your approach to project management based on the best practices identified earlier in the book. Use technology selectively to impact on performance in ways that minimise complexity, bureaucracy and cost.

People make projects successful, not technology! Reflect on each of the technologies presented and ask yourself and the team these questions:

What should we do?	What needs do we have as a project team that technology might automate or help us with?
What do we need to invest in?	What type of technology might meet our needs?
What resources will we require?	What level of investment would be required and what options are there?
What is the timing?	When would be a good time to introduce the new technology – is there is a 'window of opportunity'?

Visit www.Fast-Track-Me.com to use the Fast Track online planning tool.

Improvisational working within projects

Professor David Birchall

There is a view that the management of project-based work is moving away from the traditional paradigm of 'plan, then execute the contents of the plan' to something rather more organic and less mechanistic. Specifically, there is a realisation on the part of project and other managers that all work is different, being affected by constantly evolving and changing external influences and the dynamics of an increasingly turbulent organisational environment.

Essentially, adherents and exponents of project-based work are waking up to the idea that organisations are complex, adaptive environments (see the work of Ralph Stacey for more on organisations as complex adaptive systems[1]), where the routines and frameworks that were applied 'last time' may not suffice to solve or resolve the issues encountered in the current project. Competent and/or progressive project managers are therefore 'improvising' in order to meet current requirements.

Improvisation has been defined in a number of ways, including 'the conception of action as it unfolds, by an organisation and/or its members, drawing on available material, cognitive, affective and social resources'.[2] The inference here is that deciding what to do and doing it are almost simultaneous, and in reality, experienced improvisers draw on a personal library of improvisational interventions that have worked before in other instances and amend them to fit new circumstances.

Many of the ideas that underpin improvisational work come from literature on organisational 'sense-making' (the work of Karl Weick is influential here), and in the latter part of the 1990s the components of improvisational working were identified. Essentially, the first three key elements are: **creativity**, involving an element of lateral thinking to devise a resolution; **intuition**, in that often action is based on a 'gut feeling' for what will work in a particular situation; and **bricolage**, a lesser-known element that basically involves 'doing the best job you can with the resources you have at hand'. Bricolage is important because project managers do not tend to have time to mobilise additional resources when conceiving and executing actions contemporaneously.

Four additional components have since been developed. These are:

[1] Stacey, R.D. (1996), *Complexity, Creativity and Management*, San Francisco, CA: Berrett-Koehler.
[2] Cunha, M.P., Cunha, J.V. and Kamoche, K. (1999), 'Organizational improvisation: what, when, how and why', *International Journal of Management Reviews*, 1 (3), 299–341.

adaption, defined as the adjustment of a routine or action to new or different conditions; **compression**, usually involving simplification or shortening of steps to save time; **innovation**, requiring deviation from existing practices or knowledge; and **learning**, which triggers or informs a systematic change in future behaviours.

Essentially, project managers combine these elements to respond to unplanned occurrences within projects, and experienced improvisers are adept at resolving ambiguities in this way. Organisations need to devise a framework within which improvisation can happen, and that framework can be relaxed or loosened as managers develop trust in improvising employees. There is a requirement to dismantle overtly controlling management styles, in order to allow employees the time and space to try new ways of achieving their allotted tasks.

Thus improvisation is an extension of the trend towards the relaxation of control within modern organisations, allowing access to the tacitly held knowledge of experienced managers.

EXPERT VOICE

5

IMPLEMENTING CHANGE

Let's assume that up until now projects in your organisation have been poorly planned and implemented. The norm is late and over budget. That is the environment you have got to change. By 'environment' we mean either that which affects all the projects in your company or that which affects just those of your project team. In either case this integrated project management approach will be beneficial. It will involve putting in place processes that are new to people and asking people to change, perhaps quite dramatically, the way they work. That's why it is helpful to think about change management – how do you persuade people to do things differently, particularly if in their view things have been going fine up until now?

Where late and over-budget is the norm, people really believe that it's not possible to make changes to improve performance. At least, some people do; the others are your supporters and so getting them behind you is key to managing change.

So, what should change in terms of the project environment? You might wish to use the integrated project management process (see figure overleaf) that was referred to in Chapter 3 (see page 34).

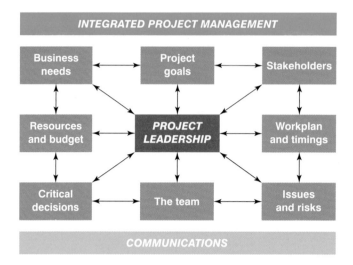

The logical starting point is the introduction of those elements of the integrated framework that are most urgently needed. We find when we go into companies that the area most team members struggle with is the very first step in the integrated approach – agreeing the business needs and the benefits the project is required to produce. So this could be our starting point, improving the ability of the organisation to reflect the business needs within all projects. If we use this as an example of how to change the project environment, you can use the audit tool from Chapter 2 to prioritise which areas to start on first.

Project team members, particularly people with a specialised technical skill, may not feel that they really need to know what the business case is or how the project is going to take the company forward. Their role, they feel, is to carry out the tasks that the project manager assigns them, and any time spent discussing things they understand little, like return on investment, they see as time taken off those tasks. If you firmly believe, as we do, that those people involved in projects deliver a better quality end result if they understand the business context in which they are operating, then you need to ensure that the business needs are integrated into every project that is done in the business.

When you have done your preparation work, call a meeting with key stakeholders to open up the discussion about the business needs. Put in place actions to be carried out by team members in all the project teams and try to gain agreement on the business needs with the functional manager for whom the project is being implemented. The key is to make sure that your opening remarks explain why understanding the business needs is a crucial part of the process for all involved:

→ **Individual team members.** Knowing more about the business is bound to increase their value to this and any other company. Unnecessary work can also be avoided if a team member realises that some activities in the plan are not driving the business needs and so can be rejected.

→ **The team.** The team is much more likely to have useful insights that help to implement the project if it understands what the functional managers are trying to achieve. After the project there is little point in boasting that your critical path analysis was proved correct; no one is interested. But there is terrific kudos in achieving the objectives of a project that makes money, provides better customer service or solves some problem that senior managers have known about for some time.

→ **The organisation.** The project is much more likely to bring real benefits to the organisation if the whole team knows the business needs and the business case.

It is often a good idea to bring the project sponsor into that first meeting to explain what the problems are in running their part of the business and how they hope the project is going to help. In our experience, those projects that get a senior business manager to spend a little time up front explaining the importance of the project are more likely to deliver on time the business value required.

Now back to preparation. Before such a meeting you will be aware of who is going to resist this fundamental change and who is likely to welcome it as an obviously sensible thing to do. The supporters we call 'change agents', and there is a good rule of thumb that says if 20 per cent of all the people affected by the change are supporters then there is a reasonable chance that you will drive the change through with their help. With less than that, it may be better to start somewhere else. This process is often called stakeholder analysis (see page 43).

> **QUICK TIP CONSTRAINTS**
> Face up to constraints in a logical fashion – use a consistent process approach to tackle problems such as severity, impact or chronology, and avoid emotional responses.

Planning the changes

Continuing with the business needs example, we now need to ensure that every project in future will include this part of the integrated framework. This can be achieved in a number of ways:

→ **In the planning meeting, insert an agenda item that details the business needs**. Ensure that all projects use a consistent template for running meetings so they all include that agenda item. Set that template up and ensure that it becomes mandatory for all projects, at the pre-planning or planning phase.

→ **Set a trigger for all project managers to identify their project sponsor and make best efforts to get them to come to the initial planning meeting with the project team**. The project manager should brief the project sponsor that their role at the meeting is to illustrate to all project members the business value of this project. This trigger should be in a standard operating procedure (SOP) guide or best practice manual for all project managers.

→ **Brief all senior managers on their role as project sponsors and the importance of relating all projects to a business need**. This needs to be factored into the SOP for appointing a project sponsor.

→ **Complete a stakeholder analysis at the earliest opportunity**. A table (like that in Chapter 3 on page 44) needs to be made mandatory and all project managers should fill it in with their core project team prior to the planning stage of the project.

→ Give change agents, i.e. those stakeholders who are advocates of the project, a formal role within the project team. Do this even if it is only to communicate the business benefits of the project within the company as a whole.

When these actions are formalised and put into either a SOP manual or a project guide, you can be confident that you have made a good start to implementing an effective integrated project management framework. However, the aim is to change behaviours, not just put words on paper, so something more is required.

 CASE STORY **INTERNATIONAL BANK, ROY'S STORY**

Narrator Roy was appointed to head up the central project management office (PMO) of an international bank, based in London, in order to put in place best practice project management principles across the organisation.

Context The bank had recently recruited a team of experienced project managers to establish a PMO, located at the head office in London.

Issue The cultural change required in the bank to adopt a common set of project management practices across a global network was massive. Additionally, anything that came from head office was viewed with some scepticism.

Solution Under Roy's leadership, the PMO created a hard copy and soft copy of a project management manual, and organised a training workshop to reinforce the use of the process. Additionally, Roy 'lent' experienced project managers from the PMO to large projects, to give physical support and so overcome the resistance from operating companies.

Learning While it is critical to capture new processes in a SOP manual, the changes must also be 'sold'.

Ensuring success

Keeping the plan on track

How do you keep track of what is going on? Once your project has been launched, your primary role as the project manager is to keep it on track. Remember the old military adage, 'No plan survives contact with the enemy' – which means that simply putting a plan together, no matter how carefully constructed, will not ensure that it will run smoothly or even at all. You need to create a feedback system, a mechanism by which you can manage and balance three distinct elements:

→ **plans** – timings and tasks

→ **people** – stakeholders and allocated tasks

→ **performance** – the objectives, goal and quality of the project.

A simple process to use is the plan-do-check-act cycle – abbreviated to PDCA. It is a continuous improvement approach to monitoring and managing a project or a team (see figure).

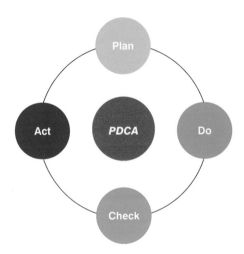

→ **Plan** your projects and deliverables – the Gantt chart, critical path analysis and work breakdown structure (WBS) are visible representations of this step.

→ **Do** the tasks, using the necessary resources.

→ **Check** all the projects' progress at the milestones or gates you have built into the plan. These are the points at which issues or problems may emerge and may require an amendment to plans. Your effort should go into managing the changes and issues rather than the actual checking progress, so the more you can automate or delegate the checking of activities, the better.

→ **Act** upon the issues raised in the checking step. This will involve new decisions, actions or re-planning – all with the aim of bringing projects back on track to meet their objectives and goals.

QUICK TIP **WORK BREAKDOWN STRUCTURE**
When creating a WBS you can use either an indented list format or an organisation chart format. The latter is useful for scoping the whole project.

Reports and routines

As part of the drive to simplify the checking process you should be look-ing to set up a regular schedule of meetings, in addition to the formal end of stage gate meetings. To make these meetings work for you, try to ensure that you have a standard template for preparing, running and fol-lowing up each meeting. Think whether your organisation has either an agenda template or a minutes template and see if you can adapt them for the needs of your change programme.

In addition to these meetings, think about briefings to keep people up to speed with progress and project issues. We have drawn a distinction here between meetings and briefings:

→ **Formal meetings** need to be planned for and factored into Gantt charts and work breakdown structures and are used to formally check progress and deal with issues that arise from monitoring performance.

→ **Briefings** can be quick and simple five-minute updates to keep people abreast of the situation. Make a distinction between the two and plan accordingly.

Leading the change

Introducing a project management framework

Remember that it is people who run projects, not systems, software or processes. To that end you need to ensure that you are flexible and responsive to the needs of stakeholders and the project team. Think about your style of management and how much leeway you give your teams in terms of making decisions and taking action.

Often this style is reflected in the detail that project managers insist upon in the work breakdown structure (WBS). The WBS is covered in more detail in the Director's Toolkit on page 179, but, in short, you need to ensure that when you plan your changes (or any projects in general) it is not done in too much detail. If you break down the project into too much detail you run the following risks:

→ **You make a rod for your own back.** Ultimately, you, as the project manager, will have to ensure that all elements on the WBS are done. So the more elements you put in, the more you will have to check.

→ **Too much detail reduces flexibility for your team.** If they already have an efficient way of doing a task on the WBS, but you have mandated more detail on *how* they should do it, then you waste this opportunity and skill. Make sure you only tell people *what* to do and not *how* to do it: one is content and the other is stylistic.

→ **Being too prescriptive demotivates people.** If you trust your staff to do a job well, then don't do the project management equivalent of standing over them!

However, there are also risks in not giving enough guidance within the WBS:

→ Not enough detail for inexperienced team members can lead to indecision and falling behind in project schedules.

→ Enthusiastic team members can do too much of the wrong thing or not enough of the right thing if the WBS and guidelines are too vague.

→ You run the risk of not meeting the project objectives if the planned tasks are too 'high level'.

Ultimately it is a balance of how much detail you as a manager insist upon, and this will be reflected in how loose or tight your management style is. The right level will come with experience and also your knowledge of the people you are working with.

As a leader, don't get bogged down by using project tools and techniques at the expense of moving the project forward. Use certain techniques if they add value but be flexible and always look for shortcuts and better ways of doing things. Often your team can be the best source of these ideas, so tap into their creative side as often as you can and don't be restricted by sticking to processes too rigidly.

QUICK TIP CONSTRAINTS
Explain the constraints and limiting factors to all who agree to take part in the project. Don't hide any constraints, but give everyone the full picture.

Managing change and resistance

To a large degree change management, for that is what this really is, is about overcoming resistance and people's fears and objections to your plan. We have found that it pays to be mentally prepared when implementing changes in a business, as not everyone will think like you. You have to deal with people's resistance to change, not try to prevent it.

To that end many successful clients have adopted the DREC curve as a means of understanding people's attitudes to changes. DREC stands

for the four 'emotions' you may come across while introducing change –
for example, a new project management framework:

→ Denial

→ Resistance

→ Exploration

→ Commitment.

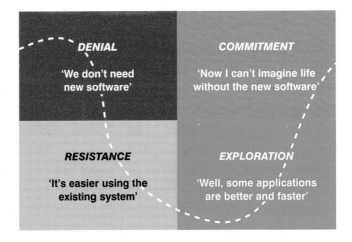

In the figure above, the statements illustrate fictional reactions to an
event, but what is important is the curve through the four quadrants.
How you manage these reactions is crucial to the smooth implementation of change. So, in the example of a new project management
framework, you could try the following strategies:

→ **Denial.** Initially the team might say, 'We don't need a project
management framework' or 'This framework will be a waste
of time and effort'. At this stage many comments are emotional and not rational and are borne out of fear of change.
Many clients inform us that it is often best to allow colleagues to get their fears off their chest and allow them a
'rant' at this stage. Your role as owner of the project is to get
through this stage as quickly and as painlessly as possible,
not to hit their denial head on, which may only prolong matters and create opponents.

→ **Resistance.** At this stage there may be a tacit acceptance of the need for change, but its relevance may be limited to the individual in question. 'The framework may be useful to you, but not for my department' or 'Well, you'll have to do it in your time and with your resources, as it's not needed by my team' are the statements you may hear at this stage. Your role as the leader of the initiative is to get resisters to understand the benefits of your approach and to get them at least to explore certain scenarios and opportunities.

→ **Exploration.** Your role at this stage is to expand the areas in which the resister might find your project management framework useful, albeit on a limited scale. It may be about selling the benefits of the framework and showing how it might solve problems for the individual. It may be about getting them to use the framework on a limited basis or piloting it for a limited time only – a taster with no commitment at this stage.

→ **Commitment.** Ultimately this is where we are trying to get people to – an acceptance that your framework is fundamental to the running of projects within the business, which in fact they couldn't do without it. However, don't look for praise or reward, as this may be another uphill struggle. Your reward should be the implementation of your initiative.

In summary, people using the DREC curve talk about the leader's role being that of getting people to the fourth quadrant as quickly and as painlessly as possible, but having to go through the three previous quadrants first. There is no jumping quadrants – no easy jump from denial to commitment. Once you understand how resistance to change manifests itself, you can focus on the process by which you implement your integrated project management framework.

Critical success factors

How can we increase our chances of implementing an effective integrated project management framework?

→ Start the change programme with a 'quick win'. 'Nothing succeeds like success', so try to pick some 'low hanging fruit' in terms of easily attainable goals or objectives. This will motivate the team. Communicate these successes widely.

→ Get active commitment from the senior management team within your business. The change programme is an internally facing project and therefore you should get some internal support. The higher the better.

→ Develop a system or process to help with reporting, monitoring and communicating. These functions are common to all types of project. Get these in order and your administrative burden as a project manager will reduce.

→ Focus on high-value objectives that fit the current business need. You know there is a need for an integrated project management framework, but what specific business issues can be resolved? These should be your focus.

→ Reward people for sharing ideas and ways of doing things. As change programmes are internally focused (as opposed to being client focused), look for ideas from all staff and reward those who come up with good ideas, irrespective of whether they are in your project team or not.

→ Use the change programme as a way of assessing the performance of your project teams. This will help you to select those to involve in important client-facing projects.

→ Develop skills to improve the quality of the work people do in project management. This will improve the overall effectiveness and efficiency of the project management framework/ infrastructure.

→ Communicate, communicate, communicate. Always and often.

→ Evaluate progress and assess performance in a regular, standard way.

→ Learn from your failures as well as your successes. Keep a 'lessons-learned' log to help the project team and to improve every project you do.

QUICK TIP **MONITORING**

Monitoring the project is a constant task. Have a good reporting process set up from day one, as problems can occur at any time along the way.

STOP – THINK – ACT

After reading this chapter you will be aware that implementing an integrated project management approach or methodology is not necessarily quick or easy. It needs to be planned and implemented using a disciplined approach. Use the team audit in Chapter 2 to identify the gaps in your current approach to project management (note that there is a more comprehensive team audit in the Director's Toolkit on page 173). Then identify the actions you will need to take to make your project succeed.

What should we do?	What stages and tasks are appropriate?
Who do we need to involve?	Who needs to be involved and why?
What resources will we require?	What information, facilities, materials, equipment or budget will be required?
What is the timing?	How long will each activity typically take?

Visit www.Fast-Track-Me.com to use the Fast Track online planning tool.

Is project management a problem or an opportunity?

Professor Stephen Wearne

Project management is easy. Deliver what people need when they want it. Achieve this by questioning what they think they want, agreeing a scope and how to deliver it, applying lessons of handling the uncertainties, organising the resources needed, checking that the client is willing and ready to do what they need to do, living with them to see that they do it, preparing the customer for what they get, and always adjusting to what happens.

EXPERT VOICE

So why is project management largely 'fire-fighting' – having to find means of overcoming immediate threats to the delivery of the intended project which could have been anticipated? Questioning people on projects in the construction, manufacturing, process and service industries in North West Europe reveals that they suffer many threats to delivering projects successfully.[1] The greatest threats stem from problems of roles, communications, leadership, supervision, teamwork and trust – what can be classed as *organisational* problems. Problems of *time* and *resources* are also substantial, and after them problems of *project definition*, *cost*, *contracts* and *change*. By contrast, *risk*, *quality* and *safety* are not seen to be major problems.

The data from different sectors of industry is remarkably similar, even with different types of employer and size of project, and over 18 years of questioning. These greatest problems thus appear to be typically characteristic of project work, at least in the Western cultures represented in this data. Over the past few decades the growth in industrial and professional attention to the needs of projects indicates much more awareness of the potential problems and how to manage them. This should have reduced the impact of the problems and increased confidence in controlling them, yet these same categories of problem persist. They remain a definition of the main tasks of project management. Although the word 'unique' is used in some definitions of what a project is, many writers observe that the life cycles of all types of project are similar. So, too, may be the problems that need to be anticipated and controlled through any project.

Most of the reported problems are due to practices within organisations – institutional habits and unwise decisions. They could therefore be avoided and fire-fighting could become redundant, or at least much reduced. The first task of project management must therefore be to look at the causes of potential problems of roles, communications, leadership, supervision, teamwork and trust. Above all, this requires skills in organisational relationships.

[1] Hussain, R. and Wearne, S.H. (2005), 'Problems and needs of project management in the process and other industries', *Transactions of the Institution of Chemical Engineers – Research and Design*, 83 (4) 372–8.

CAREER
FAST TRACK

Whatever you have decided to do in terms of developing your career as a manager, to be successful you need to take control, plan ahead and focus on the things that will really make a difference. You need to ask yourself how you get into your company's key talent pool.

The first ten weeks of a new role will be critical. Get them right and you will be off to a flying start and will probably succeed. Get them wrong and you will come under pressure and even risk being moved on rather quickly. Plan this initial period to make sure you are not overwhelmed by the inevitable mass of detail that will assail you on arrival. Make sure that other people's priorities do not put you off the course that you have set yourself.

Once you have successfully eased yourself into your new role and gained the trust of your boss and the team, you can start to make things happen. First, focus on your leadership style and how it needs to change to suit the new role; then focus on the team. Are they the right people and, if so, what will make them work more effectively as a project team?

Finally, at the appropriate time, you need to think about your next career move, and whether you are interested in getting to the top and becoming a company director. This is not for everyone, as the commitment, time and associated stress can be offputting, but the sense of responsibility and leadership can be enormously rewarding.

You've concentrated on performance up until now – now it's time to look at your Fast Track career.

THE FIRST TEN WEEKS

The first ten weeks of starting a new role as the leader of a project team are probably the most critical – get them wrong and you risk failure, get them right and you will enjoy and thrive in your new role. What do you need to do, where should you focus and what must you avoid at all costs?

For most people project management is a 'part-time' role. By that we mean that they are asked to manage a project, or series of projects, in addition to their day-to-day function. There are also many people who are full-time project or programme management professionals, in which project management is their core discipline. If you are a person new to managing projects, as well as coping with your usual activities how are you going to make a difference within the first ten weeks?

Let us answer that by asking another question – what happens if you don't make any progress within the first ten weeks or, even worse, make progress in the wrong direction? If your answer to that question is that such a situation is unthinkable, you now need to ask yourself the following:

→ What do I need to do?

→ Where should I focus my effort and attention?

→ What must I avoid at all costs?

As a new Fast Track manager, you will need to understand key facts, build relationships and develop mechanisms for monitoring and control – establishing simple but effective processes for understanding how things are progressing and what line managers are focusing on. Modern technologies can simplify these tasks, but there is no substitute for getting to know people and forming good working relationships with individuals and creating a supportive culture.

The best example of this we've come across was a new sales director for a telecoms company in the UK. We had known him some years before in a different corporation. One day we saw him on the fire escape, pipe in hand, talking to the smokers who used the fire escape as their smoking area. In a quiet moment we asked him when he had taken up smoking a pipe. 'I haven't,' he said, 'I just use it as an excuse or prop to allow me to get in with the smokers on the fire escape.' When asked why he wanted to do that, he stated that the smokers were often the best-informed people in the organisation because they spent their smoke breaks discussing business issues and rumours across almost all the functions. He had created an informal network from the tobacco addicts on the fire escape. He never actually lit his pipe and we're sure that the smokers twigged his game, but we think they appreciated a senior manager standing out in the cold discussing business with them.

In your new role, you may need to choose and use differing leadership styles based on specific project situations. Making the right choice is a skill that will come with experience. Many people new to project management believe that because they have been given the role of 'project manager' and have a copy of the latest scheduling software, people will do their bidding automatically. Nothing could be further from the truth. People make projects successful, not software or systems. Developing working relationships is a vital first step in your 'career' – either part-time or full-time – in project management.

CASE STORY *GERMAN SPECIALITY CHEMICAL CORPORATION, CHRIS'S STORY*

Narrator Chris was brought in as a consultant primarily to help with improving marketing projects, but the principles he used there were readily adopted by other departments. He was then asked to review projects at a more strategic level using a flexible tool set.

Context A German speciality chemical company had been spun off from its parent company and the owners (a merchant bank) were keen to raise the value of the company before a corporate sale or flotation on the stock market.

Issue Great pressure was exerted to speed up the delivery of projects in order to raise the value of the business before a trade sale or flotation. All projects were fast-tracked. However, the focus was so much on doing things 'by the book' that project managers had taken their eye off the business need. For example, a new chemical was released to market that was effectively obsolete because a competitor had recently launched a similar product.

Solution Despite the pressure for rapid results, Chris identified that all projects had to be linked to present market needs and meet customer requirements exactly. If this meant bending the methodology of project management slightly in order to do the right thing, then so be it: relevant business objectives must be central. Chris recommended that all project managers should fill in a project passport identifying the business/market need – this should then be updated monthly.

Learning The culture of the company was one of rigid adherence to principles and procedures, even at the expense of doing the right thing. Project managers had to learn to be flexible in their approach and keep an eye on the marketplace.

Changing roles

Why is this a critical time?

Whenever you start a new role or job, whether within your existing business or joining a new company, you have an opportunity to make a positive impression on others. However, remember that you will only get one chance to make a first impression[1] – get the first few months wrong and it could impact your relationships with others for a very long time. While working in the NHS, Simon came across a project manager with the nickname 'Shouty'. He asked whether the nickname was supposed to be ironic, as the manager seemed to be the most placid and calm of all managers in the NHS Trust. Simon was told that when Shouty had first joined the Trust he had a habit of barking orders to people. When Simon asked how long he had been there, the reply was 12 years. In fact Shouty hadn't barked an order to people in over 12 years, but first impressions stick, if only in a nickname.

During a period of transition, the team you are joining will normally have few preconceptions of you. People may have an open mind and be willing to try new ideas: they give you the benefit of the doubt. We often see this phenomenon when consultants are called in to resolve a critical business issue. The consultants often say exactly the same things as some of the internal managers, but as outsiders their views are respected and acted upon. Indeed it is an accepted, though controversial, practice to bring in consultants to recommend bad news, like the closure of a department, even though the internal managers know that it has to be done. The lesson to learn from this is that if there is going to be bad news, spend time to identify it quickly so that you can announce it before you have fully bonded with your team.

The first ten weeks are typically a period of high emotional energy, when activities will often get a higher level of enthusiasm and commitment. Use this time wisely and you will gain a significant advantage.

What are the potential pitfalls?

While this period of transition presents opportunities to make a good impression, take care not to get it wrong. Few people recover from a bad start in a new role. You will be faced with a number of challenges to overcome:

→ **You will lack knowledge and expertise in your new role.** This will make you vulnerable to getting decisions wrong. Being a good judge of character will help, as people will always offer

[1] Watkins, Michael (2003), *The First 90 days*, Boston MA: Harvard Business School Press.

suggestions to new starters and you need to decide whether to follow their advice. Ultimately, of course, you will be judged on your own decisions but look around to see whether there is someone whose judgement and assessment of other people you can trust. Take their opinions as useful input, but remember that the decisions will be yours.

→ **Getting in with the wrong people can limit your opportunities for future promotion.** In every team there will be a mixture of people and opinions, so try to understand the office politics before you join the team or department. Is the department under the microscope, expanding or readying itself for redundancies? How critical is the team to the success of the higher business unit or the company as a whole?

→ **There will be a lot to do in a short time and you may well feel overwhelmed by it all.** Prioritise, prioritise, prioritise! There are only so many hours in the day, so although you may be tempted to go in like a whirling dervish and sort everything out at once, the practical reality is you won't be able to. You need to work out what is important and make progress on those few, key issues first.

→ **Most effective managers rely heavily on their informal networks, but in the early stages of a new job these don't exist.** Judge people by their actions rather than their words. Trust those who deliver or who have a good reputation for delivering. Try to build informal networks outside your department or team, as well as sounding boards within it. The most progressive of companies now run a mentor programme for up-and-coming managers. Unlike coaching, a mentoring programme focuses on the individual within the current company context. It is not necessarily about skill development but helps the individual perform within the particular business environment in which they find themselves. If your organisation doesn't have a mentor programme, suggest setting up an informal one. Most senior managers are flattered to be asked for their advice and experience. Not only that – it's also good business sense.

What is the worst-case scenario?

Because people sometimes give new starters the benefit of the doubt, things often seem to go well for a period of time. If you make mistakes they will forgive you because you're new to the job. This is referred to as the 'honeymoon period'. New football coaches, for example, are allowed to lose the first few games without too much criticism. However, after a period of time (the first ten weeks), you, like the coaches, will need to perform well, meeting the expectations of key stakeholders and winning them over as supporters.

During this initial period, it is vital that you take the necessary steps to set yourself up for longer-term success. Otherwise you run the risk of, as it were, falling into the chasm – you make a good start but then people begin to see what you are doing as just another management initiative. You need not only to make initial gains and successes but also to sow the seeds for longer-term success. A trap that many new managers fall into is that the first few weeks of their new role is unlike the rest of their job, it is atypical, but they plan on the longer term being like the short term. Plan your first ten weeks carefully in order to set yourself up for longer-term success.

The first ten weeks

What should I do before I start?

Before starting a new project or job within the area of project and pro-gramme management, you need to do your research to find out what it will entail and what some of the potential problems are likely to be. Develop a personal to-do list of things to get ready or put in place.

Think also about how you yourself will need to change. How will you behave differently, what knowledge will you need to gain and what new skills would be useful? Understanding these things will help to build your confidence.

It is also useful, if not crucial, to identify key influencers in the project management arena, such as industry experts or your internal operations director, and start to build your reputation. Again, this is where a formal or informal mentor programme can help out.

What should I do in the first ten weeks?

When we suggest to young managers that they need to create a plan for their first ten weeks, we get many a raised eyebrow, usually from experienced managers. 'I never needed that sort of thing' is the usual comment. However, times have changed and business has never been so unforgiving. Learning on the job means exactly that – learning from mistakes and getting better with time. Since the pace of change has never been faster, now all management gurus agree that the 'learning curve' is a lot steeper.

People today expect more, faster and are less forgiving. There are always some senior managers who realise that mistakes are a chance to learn and improve, but, in our experience, they are few and far between. If you do find yourself working for a senior manager who is enlightened enough to help you learn from your mistakes as well as dissect your successes, then firmly hitch yourself to their coat-tails, as they are a rare breed indeed.

A ten-week plan is a great idea. In the numerous roles and jobs that we have had over many years we can think of many occasions where such a plan would have helped put things into some sort of perspective. We create project plans, five-year strategy plans and some colleagues even have 'life plans', so why not have a ten-week 'new job induction' plan? It makes sense to us, and if nothing else it will set you apart from the vast majority of average people out there. It sends a message – 'I'm serious about this new role and this is how I'm going to make it work.'

Use the following suggestions to put together a plan for the first ten weeks in your new position as a project manager.

Week 1: Get to know your stakeholders

First impressions influence the way a relationship develops in the first few months. Start by understanding the key stakeholders in the area in which you are working: what their roles are and how each could impact on your success. These stakeholders will typically include your boss, work colleagues, your project teams, functional heads, key opinion leaders, subject matter experts, key customers and suppliers. Knowing who they are and making a comprehensive list of them is a good starting point. If, for example, you are going to manage a project that changes how salespeople enter new sales orders, then put senior salespeople and managers on the stakeholder list, even though their actual involvement may be further down the line. You're trying to pre-empt problems here and make it more certain that you will gain acceptance of the impact that your project is going to have on other people.

Develop a communication plan that includes face-to-face discussions, to improve the support for your team from all the highly influential stakeholders. There is no substitute for face-to-face meetings. It is better to start with these meetings rather than trying to introduce your way of doing things and your suggestions from an unknown email address. However, do not go into meetings without stopping and thinking them through. If the other person feels that you have just strolled in to have an 'exploratory chat' they will also feel that you have wasted their time. If you do just want to introduce yourself, then say so, and do it outside a formal meeting. In fact many organisations used to formally walk new managers around the organisation to show their face to all in the business. This seems to happen less and less, which is a shame, since there is no substitute for 'pressing the flesh' and saying hello face to face.

What is the impression you want to give, and what do you need to do to make sure this is the impression other people will get? Think about what could go wrong and what you can do to make sure risks are avoided or mitigated. Probably the biggest risk is that you will demonstrate a lack of knowledge, so make sure that initial conversations focus on the other people and not on you. Take time to really understand what their agenda is, what their concerns are and what their ideas are for the future. Try not to state your ideas at the initial meeting – it is much better just to listen hard. Indeed it is often said that influence most belongs to the person who says least during the meeting but provides the summary at the end and proposes the action plan.

It is worthwhile assessing each stakeholder group on a power versus support matrix (see figure on the next page). Focus on those stakeholders who have the greatest power or influence over your work. Think hard about how you can win round those that will oppose your ideas and consider ways of using the support of your advocates. Remember that if you don't do this analysis you will be drawn into spending more time with people who agree with you and they may not be part of the power base you need. In effect you will be talking to the people in the green square of the influence/support matrix when probably you should be spending time with the people in the red area. By definition, it is people in the red area who can prevent your project succeeding.

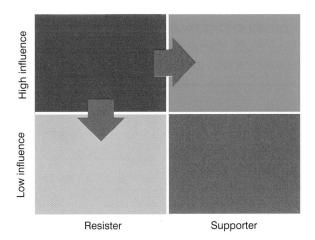

Week 2: Capture a business snapshot

You obviously need to understand the business you are working in, but this should go beyond a superficial knowledge of its products and markets. Get to know what the priorities are and the critical success factors for this current year.

You will need an appreciation of the overall strategy of your organisation in order to validate whether projects should be included in the overall portfolio – if projects are not helping your company attain its strategic goals, you have to question whether resources should be allocated to them. The test is whether you can give a confident answer to the question, 'How is your project pushing the company towards its strategic objectives and goals?'

Assess the current situation and where you think the business is. Is it a new or start-up business, or a steady-state organisation in a mature market? Is it in the process of rapid growth, a business turnaround to regain profitability, or possibly even in a wind-down phase? The current health of the business will guide the focus of your project or programme.

Your quick snapshot should also confirm what budgets and resources you already have for projects. This helps you assess the level of importance the business places on this particular activity.

QUICK TIP *USE THE COMPANY'S STRATEGY AS ONE OF YOUR CRITERIA*

To evaluate a project's fit with the company's strategy, screen projects against the key success factors.

Week 3: Create a team SWOT

Critically evaluate each aspect of your project team and identify those areas that you consider to be **strengths** and **weaknesses**, and areas that reflect **opportunities** and **threats**. Perhaps use the team audit checklist in the Director's Toolkit on page 173 to add structure to your analysis, and then summarise your thoughts in the form of a SWOT analysis.

Recognise that this will reflect your first impressions, so some of your conclusions will be valid while others may be incorrect. Take time to share your thoughts with your boss and other key stakeholders – this will provide an opportunity to get to know them better and to start thinking about ways to address weaknesses and exploit strengths. Here's an example:

Strengths	Weaknesses
CEO enthusiasm for project management Clear portfolio priorities for the current year Committed project teams with sufficient budget and time	No common project process across functional teams – inefficient and ineffective Limited visibility of current initiatives at senior level Poor learning at end of projects
Opportunities	**Threats**
Cost reduction programme could be a major programme New product development process needs to be redesigned	Poor financial performance may reduce project budget

This project manager has identified weaknesses in the way initiatives are managed across the business and the level of visibility the project portfolio has at the senior management team (SMT) level. At the same time, they believe that they have great teams and the full support of the chief executive. Perhaps a project manager in this situation might seek to use the CEO's enthusiasm to introduce some sort of project process to help give the SMT visibility and control over the project portfolio.

Week 4: Secure quick wins

Accept that you will not be able to fix everything all at once, but by week 4 people will be watching closely to see what you are actually going to do to make a difference. Make a list of your ideas for change as you progress during week 3, and then prioritise them in terms of impact on the business and urgency. Measure impact in terms of how each change will support a specific business imperative, or the difference it will make to overall profitability. Measure urgency in terms of specific deadlines that need to be met or windows of opportunity, such as, for example, implementing a process change during the summer holiday period.

For those changes that you consider to be a priority, identify one or two that you know you can implement quickly, within a few days, and with little risk. These are referred to as 'quick wins' and will do a lot to boost your credibility within the organisation – assuming they succeed. Often it is better to get a quick win of minor importance than strive for a major gain later on. The 'low hanging fruit' needs to be grabbed straight away.

Think carefully about potential problems and take time to meet with the relevant stakeholders to ensure fast success. You can then communicate these quick wins in a way that builds commitment to the overall project management programme, and builds your credibility.

For example, an effective quick win might be to conduct a one-day workshop with the different operational teams across the business, and simply capture and share their respective projects. During the workshop, ask each team participant to present their approach to managing their project, and then facilitate a discussion about the benefits of creating a common approach to managing projects, prioritisation and communication. In this way you will not only have built credibility among a key group of people, but you will also have started the process of creating common practices and increasing visibility of the overall project portfolio.

By all means report these quick wins to your boss but attribute their success to members of the team and other stakeholders. Letting your boss work out that the results were down to you rather than grandstanding your own achievements is much more powerful than hitting them over the head with how brilliant you are. You are, after all, in it for long-term career success, not just quick fixes.

Week 5: Create a vision

At the end of your first month in your new role, stop and take stock of where you are. Reflect on what you have learnt, and the key messages you have received from your boss and other key stakeholders. You should now have enough information and insights to put together your vision for at least the next year, or possibly two.

Start at the end and think about what you want to have achieved before you move on to your next role, whether it be in six months or three years. The clearer your vision of what success will look like, the more likely it is that you will achieve it. Think about how you want people to remember you after you have moved on: what will they say about you?

Then translate this vision into a team strategy or plan. This should clarify what you will do in terms of your effect on the products and services the company provides. Also decide what you're not going to do. Clarifying boundaries like this helps to focus the team and ensure that your limited project resources and budget are not spread too thinly. Then think carefully about who your customers are, whether internal or external to the business, and which are the most important. If your customers are external to the business, make sure you understand the company's marketing strategy and that your vision chimes with it.

Your vision should also clearly articulate your approach to each of the Fast Track top ten project management elements, namely:

→ project goals

→ stakeholders

→ workplan and timings

→ issues and risks

→ the team

→ critical decisions

→ resources and budget

→ business needs

→ project leadership

→ communications.

Within these elements you might identify what you see as the biggest gaps and how and when each will be closed. At this stage your vision does not need to be a detailed statement, but it should provide a roadmap stating clearly what you are looking to achieve. You will of course need to take time to validate your plan with members of the team and with your boss.

As well as putting a plan in place for the team, think about the capabilities you personally need to build in order to lead the team successfully. Where there are gaps, create your own personal development plan for gaining the necessary skills or experience. Sell this to your boss to gain their approval that you should spend the time and money to plug the gaps.

Finally, at this stage you should reflect on your new role and ensure that you are able to balance your work commitments with your preferred lifestyle. There is no point in doing a great job it you burn out in the next ten months.

Week 6: Take a break!

By the end of week 5 you will have done a great job, but you are also pretty tired. Even the most capable and confident managers tend to use up a lot of nervous energy when getting stuck into a new job.

Use this week to take time to relax and get to know the team better. Spend time with each team member on a one-on-one basis and listen to their views, their aspirations and their concerns. Get to know the whole person, not just that part of them that is involved with getting their job done. Motivating and rewarding people is much easier if you know their hobbies, eccentricities and opinions. Talk to your key stakeholders and test the various elements of your project vision, updating it as you go.

In the military it is common practice to understand the role and function of each individual under your command. That is not to say that you are expected, as a manager, to do the job better or faster than your people, but at least you should understand what the individual issues are and what motivates each team member to do a good job. This approach could be applied to any work situation. It just takes effort and time. It is our experience that this is time well spent and that individuals appreciate management time taken to understand them and their issues.

Pay particular attention to your boss, and get to know them better. What is their preferred leadership style, what are their major opportunities and threats, and how do they feel your first five weeks have progressed? How long they expect to stay in their job is an important piece of information that could impact your career path and speed of progress. Here the concept of 'managing upwards' can be useful. Realising that in large corporations your immediate boss and their boss can have a major influence on your working day, people have started to think about how they can 'manage their manager'. This is not about ingratiating yourself with your manager for personal gain – that would be a fast track to getting the wrong sort of reputation – but about understanding your immediate boss's objectives and targets. Since their actions will ultimately affect you, knowing your boss well gives you another channel by which you can understand what is happening in the business and what is in the pipeline.

During this week make sure you get on top of your day-to-day administration and clear as much of your in-box as possible. Ensure that your email list is under control and take time to delegate non-critical tasks to members of the team as early as possible. We are sure there is a direct correlation between effective personal administration and success within the first ten weeks. Some people find that setting up filing systems, mobile phone records, email folders and a diary system is second nature – it happens 'automatically' – but others have to work at it. Whatever your approach, make sure that by week 6 your personal administration is sorted and the necessary systems are in place.

If you are in a role that requires working with a secretary or PA, and this is the first time you have been lucky enough to have a secretary to work with, then it is crucial that by week 6 you have sorted out how you are going to work together. This means agreeing such things as personal phone numbers, how you work in terms of timings and diaries, how you like your diary organised, etc. Most good PAs today are experts in office management and all that entails, so get to know them and realise that they are a valuable, flexible resource that you have to manage well. A good working relationship with your secretary or PA can make or break your first ten weeks.

While working in a banking corporation we came across many managers who shared secretaries and PAs. The key to success, we observed, is to ensure that you understand how the other manager works and come to a common style and way of working. Set up an informal 'contract' of how you will work, all three of you, for best results.

Week 7: Build your reputation with others

Right, back into the fray. Recognise that your new role is fundamentally different from your previous role and that in order to succeed you may need to do things differently. This is particularly important when it is your first role in management, so you will have switched from achieving results through your own efforts and expertise to achieving results through others. Remember that your personal reputation will now be dependent on the ability of the team to deliver results. Some managers find the correct plan of action counter-intuitive. They try to take the glory for good results and blame their team for the mistakes they make. The Fast Track manager knows to do exactly the opposite: they praise the team for good results in front of senior managers and take complete responsibility for things that go wrong.

Think about the different events you attend on a weekly basis and how you should behave on each occasion. Think about what you can do to enhance your reputation for getting things done. Think about what you will get out of each event, but ask what you can do to contribute. Perhaps there are opportunities for you to take more of a leadership role or to facilitate others.

While working in a technical support call centre as customer service manager, Simon often used to bring in team members to the fortnightly management meeting to give feedback on performance and customer issues, rather than reinterpreting the information given to him and delivering it himself. Team leaders – young technical support staff – were usually given a week's notice that they would be giving feedback to senior management on the issues that had come up in the previous two weeks. After the initial panic, they were coached on their specific part of the agenda and how management wanted the data to be presented. They were shown how to distil information down into discrete chunks and not to 'tell a story'. Simon always supported them within the meeting, and management soon realised the benefit of getting information 'from the horse's mouth'.

This approach to building a team reputation with managers had some interesting results:

→ The technical support department, once undervalued, came to be seen as a valuable source of customer information.

→ The individuals within the department started to be valued more – in fact the meetings became a potential recruiting ground for the development and testing teams.

→ Simon could now leave the more repetitive aspects of the fortnightly management meetings to others, while he focused on more pressing issues and strategic tasks.

→ Individuals, once shy of giving feedback at meetings, came to see it as management 'education' and part of improving their promotion prospects; Simon saw it as succession planning; the management team saw it as just good organisation.

As a project manager your team may well not report to you directly, but could be functional specialists that come together to discuss, plan and monitor projects. These 'virtual teams' are often more challenging to lead, so in order to build your reputation you must be sensitive to the needs of individual members and understand what each function is trying to achieve. To get the best results, adapt how you work with them, talking in their terms.

Take time to build your network. The more senior you become, the more important your network will be to your future success. Your key contacts will initially be internal to the business, but as you become more established, look outside the business at professional bodies. Be critical in terms of how you use your time, as some of the network organisations you can join promise a lot but deliver little, but as a project manager in the business seek to identify and bring in best practices from other organisations.

For example, we are currently members of such bodies as the Chartered Institute of Marketing, Thames Valley Enterprise Partnership and Henley Business School Alumni Organisation. All these organisations have 'special interest groups' or areas dealing with project management and skill development for project managers in their specialist fields. These are formal organisations and associations, but we also gain much experience and learning from the less formal, personal networking groups and clubs to which we both belong. Neither of us joined formal organisations or informal groups specifically to improve our individual learning or standing in project management; we joined to meet other people and understand whether they had the same issues. However, the long-term benefits of such groups easily outweigh the odd evening having to listen to others rather than being at home. You just need to decide which groups and events will offer the most.

Week 8: Conduct your first project reviews

Your quick wins will have given you a feel for what is possible, but more importantly they will have helped to build your reputation as someone who gets things done. You will also have established relationships with key people across the business.

Now is the time to hold your first structured review of the project or projects, aimed at delivering real value to the business. Focus on a current business issue or key success factor and get the right people involved. Plan the review thoroughly and think about all the things that could take it off track. You may want to have the individuals present a brief overview of their parts of the project(s), highlighting the overall business benefits and demonstrating the link to the organisation's strategy and why they should receive the necessary resources to achieve all the project objectives.

For example, a pharmaceuticals company we knew had a project team working on the launch of a new skincare product. No one had changed the budget for the project, despite the fact that one of the key retail customers had withdrawn its order. This should have been picked up in a project review. In the same company it wasn't until we had suggested to a new programme manager that he might want to hold a strategic portfolio review early on in his new role that he discovered that two research projects, one in the USA and one in Germany, were covering exactly the same ground and were duplicating each other's efforts. A swift 'realignment' of one project saved the company millions and increased their research coverage. It also did the new manager's reputation no harm at all and his style of project review became the corporate standard for all others to copy.

The project review can be a very formal process and as a result many issues may be uncovered. It may generate more work for you and perhaps some uncomfortable decisions, but that is what it is for – not just to check progress.

QUICK TIP ALIGNMENT
Make sure that your project and the needs and priorities of the business are aligned. Are they going in the same direction?

Week 9: Reflect and learn

Now stop and review where you are. Take an hour or so at the start of the week to sit back and reflect on what has gone well, what has gone badly, and why. Go back to your original plan or to-do list and check off the items you have delivered against, and then critically review areas where you failed to meet expectations.

Meet with your boss and ask for a formal review of your progress. Many bosses are not very good at doing formal performance reviews, but nevertheless it is an essential part of continuous improvement. Then meet with your other stakeholders and get their input into what has gone well and what they would like to see changed. You may need to amend the way that you review the projects that come under your area of responsibility – how you monitor and control the progress of the various projects and how you can bring specific projects back on track.

Week 10: Develop your two-year plan

Over the last nine weeks you have built your reputation and credibility as a project (or even programme) manager, you have developed important relationships with influential stakeholders and your confidence has grown. You will by now have an opinion on what you want to achieve, based on facts and the advice of experts around the business. Now is the time to develop your two-year plan. The project reviews may substantially contribute to this as well.

Start by reflecting on your earlier vision and update it if necessary. Then work back and identify what needs to be done and achieved on a month-by-month basis. Keep the plan for year 2 at a high level, but plan the first three months in detail.

Once you have your plan, identify barriers or potential problems that could get in your way. What could go wrong, what could cause this to happen and what can you do to prevent it? Build these actions into the plan.

Finally, you should be as specific as possible about how you will know if you are succeeding. Set key performance indicators that you can monitor on a monthly basis that will let you and your boss know if you are on track. Make sure that at least one indicator tracks the financial benefits of your projects. Be clear about the business benefits that your projects are delivering, as this will help you to justify future investment in you and your team. Businesses spend money to get a return, so the project manager who cannot demonstrate the business benefits of what they are doing is the one who will feel the pinch first when times

QUICK TIP BUDGET
Ensure that your budget will allow you to complete all your activities to the quality required in the project charter.

get hard.

Checklist: what do I need to know?

During your first ten weeks in a new job, start gathering information that will help you to deliver results, build your team and develop your career. Use this checklist to see if you have the necessary information – using a simple Red-Amber-Green status, where Red reflects major gaps in current knowledge and suggests immediate action is required, Amber suggests some knowledge is missing and may need to be addressed at some stage in the future and Green means that you are on track.

TOPIC	INFORMATION	RAG
Business context	The major trends in the industry that will impact what you do, how you do it and what your project portfolio contains	
Business strategy	The overall strategy for the business in terms of its products and markets and the basis on which it differentiates itself in the market	
Team objectives	The key performance indicators (KPIs) that will be used to assess whether you and your team have been a success	
Stakeholders	Those individuals or groups that you will work with and that will influence success or failure of your project activities	
The team	Individual members of your project team – their aspirations and quirks, their backgrounds and their relative strengths and weaknesses	
Roles	A definition of the project roles and responsibilities needed to deliver results for both external contributors and those internal to the team	
Customers	Your top five internal or external customers and their specific must-haves and wants	
Suppliers	Your top ten suppliers – who they are and how they contribute to the success of your team	
Your boss	Your operational manager – their preferred style, their career aspirations and what it is that really makes them tick	
The director	The person leading project activities within the business, and possibly the person to whose job you aspire	

TOPIC	INFORMATION	RAG
Key opinion leaders	People across the organisation whose expert knowledge and opinion is respected by others – who they are and what they each have to offer	☐
Current commitments	The current operational project activities – what they are and what it will take to make them succeed	☐
Future workload	Future expectations in terms of what needs to be delivered when and by whom	☐
Budget	The amount of funding available for your project activities – where this will come from and what the sign-off process is	☐
Resources	The people, facilities, equipment, materials and information available to you for your project activities	☐
Scope	The boundaries that have been set for you and your team – the things you are not allowed to do	☐
Key events	The major events that are happening within the business that will influence what you need to do and when	☐
Potential problems	The risks you face going forward – the things that could go wrong based on the assumptions you have made	☐
SWOT	The relative strengths, weaknesses, opportunities and threats of your project team	☐
Review process	The formal review process for your internal team reviews, at which KPIs will be reviewed by your boss	☐

QUICK TIP *RESOURCES*

If resources are scarce, consider alternatives before eliminating objectives.

STOP – THINK – ACT

After reading this chapter you will be aware how critical the first ten weeks in a new role can be to success and that there are a number of actions that you should take to increase your chances of success. Change won't happen automatically and needs to be planned (like a project!). Take time now to reflect on each of these ideas and put together a plan for your first ten weeks.

What should I do?	What do I need to achieve?
Who do I need to involve?	Who needs to be involved and why?
What resources will I require?	What information, facilities, materials, equipment or budget will be required?
What is the timing?	When will tasks be achieved?
	Week 1
	Week 2
	Week 3
	Week 4
	Week 5
	Week 6
	Week 7
	Week 8
	Week 9
	Week 10

Visit **www.Fast-Track-Me.com** to use the Fast Track online planning tool.

Building knowledge networks in project management

Professor Kam Jugdev

Worldwide, the demand for project management practices continues to grow, as evidenced by:

→ the focus on project management in a range of industries, to improve efficiencies and effectiveness;

→ the increase in project complexity and the global nature of many projects;

→ the growing membership in project management associations;

→ the trend towards certification and training/education;

→ the use of project management methodologies, tools, techniques, productivity software and related collaboration products;

→ the establishment of project management offices and programme and portfolio management structures.

The emphasis on tools and techniques to control projects is important because formal and codified knowledge helps us learn *what* to do. Ensuring that project knowledge is created, shared and used is even more important when we consider that over 80 per cent of workplace learning occurs informally. *How* we practise project management is not the kind of knowledge that can be documented, as it is typically the knowledge we have learned experientially and intuitively – it is tacit knowledge. This kind of knowledge can be shared by showing others how to do things.

There are many ways in which we can engage in this informal project management learning and sharing, such as through communities of practice and our social capital. Communities of practice are founded on the premise that people engage and share knowledge because they have common interests. Communities of practice involve storytelling, coaching, showing others how to do things and mentoring. Since knowledge also flows from our network of contacts (social capital), people tend to connect with and learn from those they know, or on the basis of reputation. Additional informal ways of sharing project management knowledge include mentoring and job shadowing. A key way of sharing project knowledge involves lessons learned (project assessments), provided that these are done in a supportive environment.[2]

Informal knowledge sharing in project management will take on increased significance due to the changing worldwide demographics. Many of the 'workhorse' baby boomers (described as individuals born between 1946 and 1964) are heading towards retirement in the next decade or two. This demographic group is often described as having a strong commitment to the company. Gen-Xers were born after the baby boom generation, in the 1965–82 time period, while Gen-Yers were born in the 1983–97 time period. Gen-Xers and Gen-Yers are often described as having different attitudes towards work–life balance and management in general: they tend to want to maintain and enjoy their personal time and many expect that they will have multiple jobs and careers in their lifetime.

[2] Jugdev, K., Yurka, W., Sennara, M. and Ruwanpura, J. (2008), 'A case study on project lessons learned: the good, the bad, and the ugly', paper presented at the Academy of Management, 8–13 August, Anaheim, CA.

EXPERT VOICE

EXPERT VOICE

Given some of the different values that the generation groups have, companies face added project management challenges in ensuring that the demographic groups work effectively together. Successful project management involves a supportive organisational culture, trust, effective leadership, solid interpersonal skills and the recognition by management that its staff truly is a highly valuable resource. Companies that recognise the importance of informal knowledge sharing, together with the different needs that the generation groups have, can develop programmes that allow project teams to share their project management knowledge more effectively.

Regardless of the tools and techniques used, the key to successful project management therefore involves creating a project management culture that supports informal knowledge sharing, which can be achieved by helping each other learn *how* we practise the discipline.

LEADING THE TEAM

As you will see from the integrated project management approach we introduced you to in Chapter 3, project leadership is at the centre of all things (see figure below). Leadership is an interesting subject because there are so many thoughts on what makes a good leader and so many differing attributes and styles of leadership. In this chapter we will outline what it takes to be a project leader – as opposed to being a project manager – and what is required to build and support an effective project team.

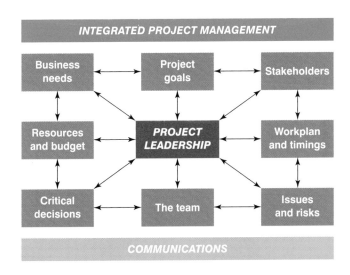

Without effective leadership, a project's chance of success is severely reduced. You can learn all the tools and techniques for effective project management, but if you do not have the ability to bring people with you and lead the project, the efforts of the team will be wasted. To date, most project management training and books have focused upon the project 'manager' as opposed to the project 'leader'. We want to change that.

QUICK TIP *LEADERSHIP*
As a project leader, don't put yourself under pressure by trying to think of everything and resolving all issues. Make full use of the skills and experience of others.

The fundamental difference between a manager and a leader is that if you have all the 'technical' skills and abilities to run a project and understand the complexities of project management as a discipline, you are probably a very good project manager, but there is something missing – a certain x factor that gives some project managers an edge. That is leadership. This difficult-to-define quality basically means an ability to bring people on a 'journey' and get the best out of them, rather than just 'use' human resources. It is leadership that affects the other axis in the matrix below – team effectiveness.

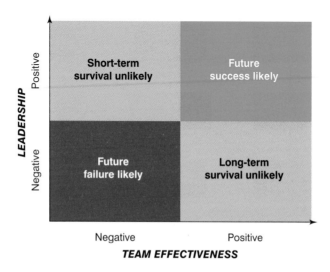

'Positive' leadership, as expressed in the matrix, is appropriate to the project situation, while 'negative' leadership is inappropriate to the situation. Leadership is a multifaceted and dynamic skill – too complex to deal with in detail in this book. So, in order to keep things straightforward, within our integrated model of effective project management we believe that the project leader should possess three basic requirements:

→ the right thinking

→ the right skills

→ the right commitment.

In this chapter we will explain what we mean by those requirements and how they can be used within a project. More importantly, we will show how you, as a Fast Track project manager, can develop such qualities too.

The right thinking

Self-perception

The starting point for managing an effective project is to manage yourself. Whenever we see a manager setting career and personal development activities for members of their team, we are often impressed by their professionalism. Unfortunately, all too often they have not been so diligent with their own personal development planning. If you are a newly promoted manager or have just been made a project manager, make sure you spend some time thinking about how you see yourself in the new role and how you wish to be seen by others. As you get into more challenging jobs you may have to adjust your thinking. Thinking differently will include not only how to deliver projects on time, to the agreed quality and within budget, but also such things as motivating team members and raising standards. Managing time, quality and budget is the starting point, but leadership requires more.

Conducting a self-assessment against four dimensions is a useful starting point: knowledge, competencies, attitudes and behaviours. Do you have the necessary **knowledge** about changes in the industry, your top ten customers and major competitors? Analysing your **competencies**, are you a process thinker, and are you able to conduct analyses to understand why things happen (or could happen), review project management processes and put into place plans that will deliver benefits on time and within budget? Do you have the right **attitude** in terms of being positive, and in your **behaviours** do you actively support others in the project management process and have the determination to overcome obstacles?

Before taking action, take time to discuss your thoughts with your boss or your coach. Perhaps summarise your thoughts in the form of a SWOT (strengths, weaknesses, opportunities and threats), before putting a plan together. However, do not be over-ambitious and try to develop yourself too quickly – becoming an effective project leader takes time.

All roles are different by nature, but the jump from one grade to the next is probably the most pronounced when you first step into management. How often do we hear people reflecting on how the ace sales representative does not necessarily make the best sales manager? This is the same for any project manager, especially as most projects involve cross-functional teams and many of the team members will not even report to you. You need to start thinking as a project management professional. While this is likely to be the most enjoyable job you will ever do, it is not something you do for the fun of it – you've got to make money for yourself and your organisation. You will also need to be more aware of the whole organisation and be proactive in terms of anticipating change. How much time do you spend thinking about the future – is it really enough? One of the key attributes of the Fast Track manager is that they will spend more time looking up and around them at what is happening in other functions or businesses.

Emphasise balance

The 'three circles', or action centred leadership model (see figure on opposite page) developed by John Adair is relevant here.[1] This simple model may not be the latest in management thinking, but good tools always stand the test of time. We have found when we are working with a client that it is often very useful for one of us to take the view of the managers and the other to take the view of the 'managed' or even the customer. This model was quite revolutionary in its day because it

[1] Adair, J. (1983), *Effective Leadership*, Aldershot: Gower.

encouraged leaders (managers) to look at things (projects) from differing perspectives – always a trait to be encouraged in project managers!

Adair's research suggested that effective leaders (or in our case 'project managers') can switch their attention and focus between the three elements of the model: the needs of the team, the task and the individual. Because all are interdependent, the leader must watch all three. Therefore, the real skill or attribute that an effective project manager should develop is the ability to know *when* to focus on the team, the task or the individual.

Applying this model to project management helps a Fast Track manager to understand where their emphasis should be at certain times or phases of a project:

→ **Task needs.** These are the objectives of the project (i.e. the needs of the business). They will be met by setting clear goals and objectives, creating the right project structure and managing the project through meetings and reports.

→ **Team needs.** These are things like effective meetings, support for stakeholders, sharing work, and communication within the team and with other project teams.

→ **Individual needs.** These will of course vary from person to person, but the effective project leader will understand how the needs of individuals in the team and the emotional needs of stakeholders should be met.

CASE STORY *CENTRAL GOVERNMENT, GRAHAM'S STORY*

Narrator Graham was a project manager within a central government IT department and was working on a major infrastructure project (he was a contractor on a long-term contract).

Context In central government IT, time spent by professionals has to be allocated to a specific project. This means that any person who is involved in a number of projects has to fill in a timesheet and account for their entire working day. Clerks then take these timesheets and input them to a system that allocates costs to the projects in the form of daily rates, as though the staff were outside contractors.

Issue The issue was that no one had any slack. Many projects were going over budget in a way that reflected the rules but not the actual contribution of the staff.

Solution Graham called the project managers together to agree an amount of time that did not need to be project-related. He then persuaded line managers to get this through the finance department.

Learning Watch out for unforeseen consequences when you take a financial system like costing out into the real world of work.

The right skills

Technical versus people

Throughout this book we have emphasised the need for good technical skills. In a project context this means the effective creation of objectives, good planning, effective management of meetings, etc. However, the project leader also needs good people skills. These people skills will inevitably be linked to a 'style' of leadership – this is *how* you interact with others. So, understanding your style of leadership is as important as understanding, say, critical path analysis or Gantt charts.

What leadership style is appropriate?

These may be your first tentative steps into management or you may be an experienced manager, but in either case take time to reflect on what leadership style may be appropriate for your role as project manager. One way of thinking about this is to consider the extent to which you involve others in events and key decisions. Project leadership is effectively a continuum from command to consensus, as shown in the figure below.

One extreme is to be dictatorial and adopt a 'command and control' style, where you make the decisions in isolation without involving or consulting others. For example, you may decide what the project tasks are and simply tell people to get on with carrying them out. At the other extreme you allow the group to decide the relevant objectives to achieve through a consensus-driven approach.

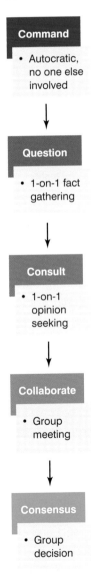

These are the two extremes of the leadership continuum and there are of course stages between the two. You may choose to ask questions of key managers in order to confirm facts, such as questioning set objectives, or you may consult them individually or as a group and ask their opinion – but then still make the decisions yourself.

So is there a preferred style for the project manager? The reality is that there is no one right or wrong answer and that your choice will vary depending on the situation. Fast Track project managers assess each situation quickly and are then flexible enough to adapt their style based on three criteria – time, commitment and quality, as illustrated below.

Time invested and speed — Commitment to decision

Quality

1 Involving others increases both the *time* delay in the decision and the number of people and time involved in the decision-making process. The extreme is 'analysis-paralysis' where projects have difficulty getting off the ground due to the perceived need to consult everyone involved at the very beginning. In addition, when quick decisions need to be made in order to react promptly to events, bringing others into the decision-making process can be counter-productive.

2 The second criteria is *commitment*. So long as the team respects their project manager, and the more involved people feel, the more likely they are to commit to decisions and actively support the implementation of the project and activities.

3 The third dimension is *quality*. There is no point making decisions in isolation if you lack the facts or experience – you will simply be risking the failure of the project and exposing your reputation as a project manager and an effective decision maker.

Reflect on your style of leadership using the involvement model. What is your preferred style? When would a consensus style be more appropriate and when would a command style be more effective? While everyone has a preferred style, Fast Track project managers are comfortable operating at all points on the continuum, but to do this they will have developed appropriate skills. Some of these skills are listed below.

→ **Command.** Ability to analyse the situation, solve problems alone, make decisions, proactively think ahead and manage risks, and the willingness and ability to tell others what to do.

→ **Question.** Ability to ask open and closed questions and, most importantly, to listen to the answers without interrupting, so that you have sufficient facts to make the decision.

→ **Consult.** Willingness and ability to listen hard to what others are telling you, noticing subtler signals such as feelings and opinions, and the ability to seek proposals from others.

→ **Collaborate.** Ability to manage meetings effectively with clear objectives, agenda and logistics, as well as a willingness to challenge the group, discuss ways forward and manage conflict where there are differences of opinion.

→ **Consensus.** Ability to set group boundaries, build consensus in a team and gain commitment to outputs, while remembering that not everyone needs to agree with the decision of the group, but that they do need to commit to it.

Coaching

While not part of the formal leadership model above, coaching should also play a role in developing yourself as well as members of your team. It is said that if you want to master a particular discipline then teach it. Fast Track managers develop excellent coaching skills – helping individuals develop core skills or resolve barriers.

The right commitment

This is not so much about your commitment as about getting the best from others. Your commitment as a Fast Track project manager we take for granted since you cannot motivate others if you are not fully motivated yourself.

Getting the best from the project team

Whether people across the business report to you or are simply contributors to your project activities, think carefully about how you will keep them motivated. First, focus on the **behaviour** you are looking for. It may be that you want people to get involved in the planning of a project or the delivery of a specific task. Whatever it is, people's behaviour will be determined by what comes before they need to do the task, called **antecedents**, and what comes afterwards, known as **consequences**:

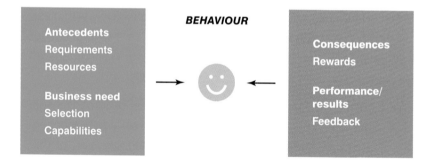

→ **Antecedents**. Once you are sure you have chosen the right people for the task, set them up for success by making it clear what is expected of them and what the outcomes should look like. Targets should be stretching but should not over-stretch individuals, as this can be demotivating. Create clear and understandable objectives and tasks. These should reflect the business need at the high level but they should also reflect the experience and skills of project members at a lower level too. Finally, think about the resources individuals will need to be effective. These may include time, facilities, materials, equipment, data and budget.

→ **Consequences.** Look closely at each task and assess the natural consequences for each person. This can be distilled down into the 'WIIFM factor'. WIIFM stands for 'What's in it for me?' If they do a great job, what happens to them or what benefits do they receive? These benefits include not only bonuses, etc. but also other elements that help motivate the individual. Avoid situations where there are positive consequences for doing a bad job. For example, if someone fails to implement a new project effectively because they are keen to move on to a different project, find a way of ensuring this does not happen. Conversely, think of ways to use consequences to drive positive behaviour. For example, if someone arrives late for the start of a project meeting, ask them to capture issues on the flip chart or to take the minutes. The most effective way of keeping people motivated is typically through the use of natural (non-financial) rewards, such as allowing them to present to senior managers, seeing a project through to completion or by you simply taking the time to say 'thank you'.

Think about the next project team meeting you will be running and use the model to check that you have set it up for success. What do you need to put in place in terms of antecedents, and what do you need to do to ensure that the consequences of participating are positive ones? For example:

Antecedents	→ Ensure that the project relates to a current business imperative → Put together an invitation to attend that includes the background, a set of objectives and an agenda with timing (allow enough time) → Invite the right people to get the right skills and ensure they understand the processes you will be using – hold a five-minute conversation with each to clarify expectations → Ensure the room you have is large enough, has plenty of natural light, encourages creativity and has the appropriate layout → Send an email reminder out a few days beforehand asking all participants to make sure the meeting is in their diaries → Think about the risks – what could go wrong – and plan mitigating actions

Behaviour	→ The team discusses and plans the project to the level of detail you have stipulated → 'Success' would be a project plan to which the team commits
Consequences	→ Ensure that the relevant stakeholders are aware of the implications of the project, specifically the resources required → Allocate a budget for a team dinner as a way of encouraging future participation and celebrating success → Arrange for someone else to capture the outputs and circulate them to the team within a couple of days → At the end of the meeting thank everyone for their contributions, picking out one or two people for particular praise

Create the right environment

Why is this important?

You and your team may be developing highly complex project plans, but without a supportive culture key stakeholders will not 'buy in', and your project will become just another initiative that quietly disappears. Even though you've given the new project the best chance of success by following a professional process and gathering the right data, you still have to take key individuals with you or your project will quickly fall apart.

An environment that is suitable for effective project management depends on the culture you create as the leader of your team and the physical environment that people work in. Both must work together to support the creative generation of ideas and the rigorous implementation of projects – for project management to flourish and be a success, both of these components are necessary.

What culture is best?

There is no one right answer to this and it will vary depending on your preferred style and the business context or situation at a point in time. The organisation may have one culture and the team may exhibit another culture. However, there are basic components that tend to result in an environment that will be more conducive to good project management, irrespective of the culture that dominates in your organisation. These include:

→ **Creative challenge.** Create an environment of challenge and confrontation, but make sure that it is positive. It is easy to knock a contribution, but make sure when you or a member of the team does that you have an alternative or are prepared to search for one.

→ **Blame-free.** When trying to scope projects there is always a degree of uncertainty and risk. This means that people will not always get it right, and not all ideas will be good ideas. Where bad ideas are heavily criticised, people quickly stop putting forward new concepts or ways of improving projects, for fear of being ridiculed.

QUICK TIP *RESPONSIBILITY*
Ask whoever is responsible for an activity or group of activities to give you their estimated start and end dates, and hold them to these.

→ **Ethical boundaries.** Make a choice about what you will and will not be prepared to consider. As well as making a statement about your beliefs – what is right and what is wrong – you will also clarify the boundaries for others. In any industry there will be the possibility of cutting corners, flirting with legality and, for example, behaving in a more or less environmentally green manner. Think about the issues that affect you and your industry and make decisions on the limits you will set. These set the tone for how you will manage other people, as well as manage projects.

→ **Learning organisation.** Work hard to create a culture where people learn from each other and from past projects. There is nothing more demoralising than running a project that fails, only to find that someone else had already made the very same mistake several years earlier. This is a discipline that needs to be built into the culture of the team. A lessons-learned database for projects is not just a technical requirement for an effective project management office but it also helps to build up the people-skills culture necessary for continuous project improvement.

The role of the project management office

Most organisations do not have a project management office (PMO), so a lot of project management activity takes place in the normal course of events – for example, when a salesperson is meeting a customer or when people are chatting over the coffee machine or having a drink after work. In contrast, in larger organisations there is a place for a project management office.

Some of the key functions fulfilled by this office are:

→ coaching and developing new staff – providing a centre of project excellence within the business;

→ facilitating project teams in project planning and problem solving – providing a source of advice and support;

→ facilitating the formal review of the project or portfolio by a project review group (this process is aided significantly by having the right facilities and equipment constantly at hand, and the more advanced organisations will have a dedicated facility for this purpose);

→ managing resources across the portfolio;

→ ensuring consistency between projects in terms of systems, etc.;

→ formulating project strategy and approach;

→ scanning all projects;

→ sharing project best practice within the business.

In the PMO the project portfolio will always be visible and keep individual projects aware of the bigger picture. Journals and books will provide access to the latest project management thinking, as well as proven techniques. There will also be an online business library – providing electronic reports covering every aspect of project management as a discipline. The standard project management process will be presented in the form of a flowchart, and there will be checklists and templates covering all subsequent projects. Finally, while the facility encourages a systematic approach to project management, there will be an opportunity for innovation and creative thinking. The office will also encourage insights and learning from project successes and failures, receiving and sharing knowledge across the teams.

Depending on the group, you may choose to use a computer with mind-mapping software connected to a projector screen, or you may choose to use Post-it notes stuck to the wall. In either case, make sure that the process of capturing, consolidating and screening the ideas does not get in the way of new thinking.

Make sure the vital rule of team planning is in place – the team leader must not impose their thoughts on the team. In fact the best idea may well come from the most junior member of the team – after all, they are the people least likely to believe that the way we have done things for years must be right. If the team doesn't think they will be listened to unless their view accords with that of the leader, they will soon stop contributing.

Building the team

What makes a great team?

So you have a great leadership style that is flexible enough to cope with different project stages and situations, and you have a number of highly motivated and skilled people to work with, but that does not necessarily make them a great team. So what do successful project management teams do that differentiates them from average performers? Read through the following checklist and reflect on what you need to do as leader of the team in order to ensure success.

→ **The team will have great clarity in its goals and have a real sense of purpose.** Fast Track teams will have such clarity of vision that they will know how they want to be remembered long after they have been disbanded. The basic differentiator between a 'group' and a 'team' is a common and enthusiastically agreed goal.

→ **The team will have a strong and enthusiastic leader.** This leader provides direction, is supportive of team members and is willing to shoulder responsibility when things do not go according to plan. They are often not the expert or specialist, but they understand how to bring experts together and get them to perform effectively as a unit.

→ **Fast Track teams also accept that things will change and can act flexibly in order to bring things back on track.** They are willing to reappraise situations quickly but calmly, explore creative options for dealing with possible changes and move on.

→ **They will have shared values and a common set of operating principles.** While teams comprise people with a variety of skills and experiences, they need to be unified by common beliefs. Shared values will often provide the team with enormous energy and commitment.

→ **Ideally, the shared values then extend into a general respect and liking for each other where members of the team trust each other and genuinely have fun working together.** The Armed Forces will always ensure that their teams spend time gaining shared experiences in a safe environment before they are asked to put their lives on the line.

QUICK TIP TRUST

Make sure that the core project team is composed of people you really trust. When the pressure is on, you need to be able to rely on them totally.

→ **There will be issues to deal with, but the Fast Track teams will manage these quickly and sensitively before they become crises.** To do this they need to have open and honest communication and work in a blame-free environment.

→ Finally, the team will be balanced in terms of the skills and capabilities of team members and in terms of the roles they each fulfil. The team will have people capable of creative challenge, but it also needs people willing to get their heads down in order to put the work in and deliver the results. You may want to allocate them roles reflecting different ways of thinking, as illustrated by Edward de Bono's 'six hats' (see figure below).[2] You may not wish to allocate these roles, but reflecting on which of your team members operate naturally wearing one of these hats will help you to make the most of your people and plug potential gaps.

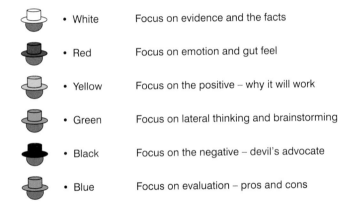

	• White	Focus on evidence and the facts
	• Red	Focus on emotion and gut feel
	• Yellow	Focus on the positive – why it will work
	• Green	Focus on lateral thinking and brainstorming
	• Black	Focus on the negative – devil's advocate
	• Blue	Focus on evaluation – pros and cons

Frequently, project teams operate as a 'virtual team', working across functions and geographic boundaries. In these cases the principles of good teams become even more important, since the influence of the leader is dissipated either by hierarchical control or geographic distance.

How should I develop the team?

As well as developing the skills of individual members of your team, you need to build them into a strong and effective team. Review the list of attributes of a great team above and make a note of any area where you feel there is a need for improvement.

---

[2] de Bono, Edward (1986), *Six Thinking Hats*, Harmondsworth: Viking.

Next, assess where you think the team is now in terms of its stage of development. This is particularly important for those working in the area of project management, as teams are often part-time – coming together for events such as project team meetings or the implementation of an initiative. Each team will go through various stages of development, and your role as the leader will be to recognise where they are and to take action to move them to a state where they are their most productive. Consider the following model:[3]

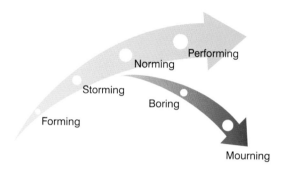

STAGE	DESCRIPTION	LEADERSHIP ACTIONS
Forming	The group is brought together for the first time and needs to spend time understanding each other and what they are each contributing. This is typical of an initial project team meeting. The team comprises members from a variety of functions that do not usually work together.	Think carefully about whom to involve in each potential team and make sure there is a balance in terms of different roles, skills and experience. Allow people to get to know each other personally and set simple tasks to allow people to work together for the first time and get a quick win.
Storming	Initially they will each be keen to contribute and will want to have their say in terms of who fulfils which role and who will have the greatest sway over the outcomes. If this is not managed carefully, the group can become very 'political', where individuals jockey for power and positions. This can result in a downward spiral in terms of effectiveness.	Make sure that the early tasks the group undertakes are straightforward and will result in success. Establish roles and communicate them clearly so that everyone knows what their contribution is. There will always be the potential for conflict, so look for it and seek consensus on key decisions at an early stage.

[3] Concept developed by Bruce Wayne Tuckman in the short article 'Developmental sequence in small groups', 1965 (**www.infed.org/thinkers/tuckman.htm**).

STAGE	DESCRIPTION	LEADERSHIP ACTIONS
Norming	As things settle down, the team will need to adopt norms in terms of how it works together. This needs to cover decision making, communication and meeting disciplines. Without common processes a lot of the energy and enthusiasm of the team can be dissipated.	Be clear about what will happen at each meeting and that there are agreed objectives, an agenda with timings and appropriate resources. Communicate your leadership style in terms of the circumstances in which you will seek the team's views.
Performing	The team should now have clear roles and be working effectively as a unit. This is where results are produced, and you need to keep the team in this positive and effective mode. It is consciously now a team rather than a group.	Monitor performance regularly and take swift action to resolve issues before they become crises. Spend one-on-one time with each member of the team to keep them motivated.
Boring	For teams that have been together for a long time, there is a danger that they stop challenging the way they work. This is common on major projects where individuals can easily get into a rut. If left unnoticed, this can result in the team getting bored, and performance can quickly fall off.	Find ways of constantly challenging the team as a whole and as individuals. Consider bringing in new members or rotate jobs and roles. Perhaps there will come a point where you need to fundamentally adjust the team's objectives in order to get them to stop and re-evaluate what they are doing.
Mourning	Finally, for high-performing teams, there is always a major sense of loss when a valued member moves on. Even if their replacement appears to have the right profile, there can be resistance, and the team effectively moves back into the 'forming' stage.	When people leave the team, for good or bad reasons, think carefully about the transition. Focus on some of the softer people issues within the team – not simply on updating the plan.

QUICK TIP OBJECTIVES

Be as ambitious as you can, but avoid committing to the impossible. There are 'stretch goals' and there is the 'impossible'.

In summary

Project management is too often seen in terms of 'hard', technical skills and people are trained accordingly. However, increasingly businesses are realising that it is people skills that are key to the success of projects – it is people who make projects successful rather than systems and processes. So, although we have talked about project 'management' and have referred throughout this book to the Fast Track project 'manager', what we want to stress is the necessity to become a project 'leader' as well (or instead). This subtle difference encapsulates the people skills required for effective project management.

In this chapter of the book we have consciously avoided referring to these people skills as 'soft' skills. This is because we have found in our many years of managing people, both in and out of projects, there is nothing soft about managing people. In fact, it is probably the hardest thing as a Fast Track project manager that you will encounter.

STOP – THINK – ACT

Reflect on how well you are leading the team and look for ways you could improve. This will be key to your success, as you will not be able to achieve your objectives working alone, and in the area of project management, project implementation is often achieved via cross-functional teams where you will not necessarily have direct control over people.

Think about how well the team is operating. Where is each individual in the 'forming to mourning' model? Think also about which groups affected by the change are not in the 'committed' section of the DREC model.

What should we do?	What actions do we need to take to build the team?
Who do we need to involve?	Who needs to be involved and why?
What resources will we require?	What level of investment would be required?
What is the timing?	What deadlines do we need to meet?

Visit **www.Fast-Track-Me.com** to use the Fast Track online planning tool.

P2M, the methodology that supports the construction of complex business infrastructures

Professor Christophe Bredillet

In the 1990s Japanese companies experienced a deflationary depression called the 'lost ten years'. To survive the depression and struggling to regain their global competitiveness, they looked for solutions in the *kaikaku* (reforms) of business management, organisations and technology. We have observed that the companies that utilised the intellectual property of the entire organisation and offered intangible benefits were more successful in their reforms than those who focused purely on their technological capabilities. Specifically, such successful companies made efforts in the planning and execution of strategic businesses that would change the framework of value creation for the next generation. These companies had something in common: they applied a new project management paradigm and related framework. We call it 'kaikaku project management' (KPM). Based on previous observations, findings and the KPM paradigm, a new Japanese framework for project and programme management – called P2M: project and programme management for enterprise innovation – was developed in 2000–1 and has since been used as a standard guide for education and certification.[4]

The programme management in P2M is a methodology to support managers in constructing complex infrastructural systems to realise intangible value and benefits, as well as in executing projects within more traditional hierarchical systems. In this approach, integration management is at the core of programme management. The process of integration management is first to clarify business strategy, then to develop a set of projects to be executed autonomously, and finally to integrate their implementation processes. Programme managers always have to face a dilemma of simplifying the concept – seeking the essence of programmes in the first phase – and then designing complex systems in the later phase. To create new value always means uncertainty, thus risk is inherent in the nature of programmes and has to be taken into account throughout integration management.

[4] Bredillet, C. (2007), '"Kaikaku" project management: investigating the Japanese answer to the 90s depression' in the proceedings of European Academy of Management (EURAM); Bredillet, C. (2009), 'Scientific Theory of Project Management' in S. Ohara and T. Asuda (eds), *Japanese Project Management: A New Project Management Paradigm*, London: World Scientific Publishing.

EXPERT VOICE

P2M institutionalises a new way of apprehending programme and project management, proposing a flexible and adaptable framework grounded in a balanced, integrated perspective combining both a rational and a creative view of the world. Going far beyond most of the existing standards, P2M offers a clear linkage between strategy (vision and mission) and the way of implementing it through programmes and projects. It provides a flexible and adaptable framework, not just a 'one best way' anchored in a Western positivist, rationalist paradigm for doing things. P2M clearly differentiates programmes into projects and their hierarchy. It proposes a specific approach to address programmes and projects. Furthermore, project and programme management governance is the management system that enables answering and acting on the demands of a wide range of stakeholders for increasingly high levels of accountability and performance. Here, governance is based on two criteria: accountability and performance. Accountability is promoted through transparency and performance is promoted by responsive and responsible decision making. P2M has included these dimensions in the whole framework. The organisation's competencies are seen as the most relevant driver for competitive advantage and the creation of value. P2M recognises that competences and learning are at the heart of value creation. In conclusion, learning and practice are integrated – the emphasis is placed on what appear to be some of the main strengths of P2M:

→ Templates are provided for ready retrieval of standard practice patterns.

→ Standard frames are built on industry lessons learned, accumulated through the experiencing–memorising–recalling–applying cycle, which helps acquire judgement capability.

→ Project professionals build professional competencies by repeating deduction, prediction and application, following the standard frameworks provided.

→ Cases in P2M facilitate analogically situated experience and simulated learning.

→ The framework is designed to enable a contextual, analogical and situational application and experience, and continuous or gap improvement.

8

GETTING TO THE TOP

We firmly believe that project management as a discipline is no longer a specialism limited to either the engineering or IT function. Historically these two areas have been the 'home' of project management, but as companies realise the need to deliver value in all things, project management has become a mainstream skill for all managers, irrespective of sector, discipline or management level. Today we believe that there are two separate paths down which managers new to project management could go.

1 **The first option is that of a full-time, 'professional' project manager.** If that is your chosen route and you wish to make project and programme management your chosen area of expertise, then you should look towards getting some sort of accreditation through bodies such as the Association of Project Managers (APM) or the Project Management Institute (PMI). Find out what is appropriate for you and take steps to move towards becoming a professional full-time project manager.

2 **The second path is to develop your project management skill or expertise, without it becoming your central job or role.** Here, you develop your project management expertise within the context of your current job area. For example, it could be becoming more experienced in project management within marketing or sales or in customer services. Those job areas will probably

guide your promotion and job path, but well-developed skills in project management will be a distinguishing factor that will help you stand out amongst your peers. It is no less professional than option 1, but the career development path differs greatly in terms of emphasis and qualifications.

The drive for performance

Whether they opt for full-time project management or use project management skills as part of their job, Fast Track managers should know what is important and what is not. They focus on the key performance indicators (KPIs) that have the greatest impact upon the business. They regularly take time to reflect on the past in order to learn from what went well or what could be improved, and they think ahead to the future so that concerns can be resolved before they become crises. By always delivering against expectations, they stand out from the pack and will be automatic considerations for promotion at the appropriate time. This is, of course, true for all disciplines and areas of expertise, but getting a reputation for delivering results, on time and within budget, is critical for project leaders.

 QUICK TIP RESOURCES
Always be prepared to justify your choice of resources, dates and budgets with relevant, factual project data.

Review past performance

In terms of driving performance in the business and getting to the top in your chosen area of project management, our experience tells us that an understanding of past performance is a very good starting point. Without an understanding of what has worked well and what hasn't, we run the risk of reinventing the wheel and making unnecessary changes – all of which will not do our reputation any good at all.

As a Fast Track project manager you should review, at a macro level, how your projects and the company as a whole have performed over the last strategic period – say two to three years. What is the trend and what are the specific problems holding back projects or performance? Ask yourself how you are going to gather that information and how others will be able to learn from it. This review or 'audit' should suggest where you can work to improve performance in the area of project and programme management in the future.

Current priorities

Having seen what has happened in the past, it may be worth looking at current initiatives and whether the so-called 'performance gap' will be closed. Those involved in managing projects and programmes will need to understand the following:

→ What programmes are underway to improve project management performance?

→ What projects are underway and what is their likelihood of success – i.e. are they on track?

→ What mechanisms are in place to deal with any project issues that arise?

Relate these findings to the audit data found previously (see Chapter 2). Is there a trend? To get to the top within project management within your business, you do need to address the environment in which projects and programmes are delivered, as well as ensuring that the individual projects you are managing are successful.

Future intentions and actions

By taking a view wider than that of simply improving individual projects – that is, engineering the project environment in which your projects operate (as discussed in Chapter 5 of this book) – you will be taking a longer-term, strategic view of project and programme management. This has benefits out of all proportion to the effort invested in assessing past projects and planning new ways of doing things. It is precisely this approach that marks out strategic thinkers against other competent project managers. Always be thinking about how to improve the way projects are managed – the process – as well as how to deliver the value of an individual project – the content.

At the top of the business, directors are always encouraged to take the longer view and to think in terms of improving processes rather than projects. For the Fast Track project manager, this is always a good tip to follow, if you want to get on in the future.

Invite challenge

Constantly challenge yourself

Business never stands still and as individuals, developing new skills and abilities, we should not stand still either. The easiest thing to do is to rest on one's laurels, but in modern business it is a reputation for driving change that is sought after and valued. Look for ways to introduce challenge to you and your team on a regular basis, aiming to bring in ideas, tools and techniques from recognised leaders in the area of project and programme management.

When possible, set up systems or processes to gather and glean information from different groups. Consider groups that may not think like you and may have a different 'take' on how your projects should be managed or approached. These could include:

→ **Other departments and teams within your company**. In a large organisation there may be other teams managing projects very successfully, using systems, techniques and processes unknown to you. We are constantly amazed how many times companies have multiple processes and systems for managing projects and programmes that are not communicated within the business. As consultants we often start by asking questions internally, and as often as not the answer can be found, in some format or another, within the business. People don't communicate best practices or even good practices for a variety of personal, organisational or political reasons. Creating an internal 'community of practice' (CoP) where you can share ideas (good, bad or indifferent) is a great way to challenge yourself and your own thinking.

QUICK TIP *SELLING NEW PROJECTS*

Make a feature of a new project so that people know it is happening. Use sales techniques within the company to 'sell' the project to staff and managers.

→ Customers. Have you ever thought about how customers manage their projects? Maybe a customer or client out there is an expert in a certain field or area of project management. You may only see them as a purchaser of your products or services but there may be more to the relationship than meets the eye. Move away from this one-dimensional view of your customer and look at them as a project partner (when appropriate) – it may pay dividends. For example, Patrick recalls a large multinational bank's PMO (project management office). They were the guardians of the bank's project management process and organised training events as well as the publishing of the project management guide for the bank. They were very happy for any client or supplier of theirs to understand and/or adopt their systems and processes, since they viewed this as a means of working more closely with a client.

→ Competitors. What are your competitors doing now that could be copied? How are you going to get that information? Many people forget that when new hires start work in your business they are a rich source of information. However, they are often only quizzed on their content expertise (*what* they know) and not on past employers' systems and processes (*how* they did things). Don't be precious about using other people's approaches to managing projects. Customise, beg, borrow and rework – all are valid tactics when trying to improve the management of your projects and programmes.

→ Supply chain. Just as customers may have a good way of doing things, your suppliers may have too. In fact many businesses actively seek to align core business processes to improve the supply of goods and services to the marketplace, and aligning your project management process to that of your suppliers is an ideal way of getting synergies and benefits. We have seen many examples where adopting the project management process of a core supplier as your own is a quick-start way of creating your 'own' project management process. With online project reporting tools and projects that include many supplier tasks and inputs, projects can be speeded up and risks greatly reduced if there is a 'symbiotic' relationship or association between suppliers and the supplied.

→ **Industry experts**. What are the experts recommending for your business sector? What breakthrough tools and techniques have they developed? Have you linked up with special interest groups (SIGs) within project management bodies such as the APM and PMI? Here you are looking for content knowledge (what?) as well as project management process knowledge (how?).

How do I keep up to date?

As well as working with other groups inside and outside the business, think carefully about what additional sources of knowledge and insight you want to receive and how often. There is a wealth of information available from a variety of sources, so you need to be selective, as the time you have available for reading is limited and the quality can be variable. Keeping up to date should not be a chore or burdensome, so being selective and specific is key. Too much searching and too much 'data' (as opposed to 'knowledge') can rapidly become distracting and diverting.

There are numerous places to look for information on the latest in project and programme management. Select a few tried and trusted sources and try to be specific in terms of the information you are searching for. Most online websites have a mechanism by which you can ask for new postings or information to be emailed to you at a certain frequency – monthly, weekly or even daily. Look for the following sources:

→ **Journals or trade magazines**. There are some standard publications in the area of project management that will often have information on latest thinking or tools and techniques. But also look for trade journals in your area of business or sector and see if they have sections on project management too. *Fast*

Track-recommendation: try to get your company to subscribe to one journal of greatest relevance for one year and then review its value. Make sure you circulate it within the company once you have read it.

→ **Conferences**. These provide a useful source of usually new information. They are also good places to network. However, they can be very time consuming and expensive. *Fast Track recommendation: it pays to get the conference agenda in advance and cherry-pick the sessions that are of the most interest and relevance to you. Aim to identify those people who are relevant to your issues and plan to follow up with them afterwards.*

→ **Communities of practice (CoPs)**. These are online discussion forums between like-minded people within specific areas of the project management 'community'. *Fast Track recommendation: these can be extremely useful or a complete waste of time, so give them a go and see what value you get. Many CoPs in project management are focused around certain software platforms or specific methodologies, so beware of being involved in something too specific too early on, as their relevance to you might be limited. You may also want to consider forming your own forum, but remember that you will need to put in the necessary time and effort to get it off the ground.*

→ **Web**. This provides freely available information from many sources, but it is usually unstructured and potentially distracting as you wade through the mountains of unrelated material. *Fast Track recommendation: treat searching the internet as a serious activity and not as surfing. Be specific with your searches and set yourself specific timescales to gather information. Once you have found useful sites, bookmark them and become active within the site by asking for information and providing comments or data.*

→ **Professional bodies**. The more senior you become, the more important and useful these bodies can be to you and your organisation, as they are often a source of free advice and networking. *Fast Track recommendation: once you have been in your role for at least a year, sign up for an initial trial period and see what benefits you receive. Gather information from third parties about the rival membership organisations and look at independent sites for recommendations. In the world of project management, the APM and PMI are two very good starting points, but do your own research. There are many smaller groups focusing upon specific project management areas.*

→ **Personal networks**. Never underestimate personal networks. Many a time we have received cutting-edge advice and information from individuals whom we would never have thought about contacting through any of the above ways. Many of these individuals are on the intersection between academia and practice and most, if not all, are self-employed. The increasing propensity for experienced individuals to work on their own as contractors in a 'portfolio career' has generated a whole workforce of experienced individuals who are not obviously affiliated to professional bodies, websites or CoPs. *Fast Track recommendation: networking always pays off.*

→ **Fast-Track-Me.com**. All the key ideas, tools and techniques contained in the Fast Track series are available via the internet at **www.Fast-Track-Me.com**. *Fast Track recommendation: firstly, allocate 30 minutes to visit and explore the site. It contains a rich source of tips, tools and techniques, stories, expert voices and online audits from the Fast Track series.*

Remember that, whatever your source of information, to maximise the benefits you need to put time aside and make the necessary effort. However, also recognise that you will never have perfect knowledge – particularly in the area of project management, as it is such a wide and expanding area of expertise. Decide what level of information will be good enough and then act on it. In our experience the best project managers and directors have their own trusted circle of advisers, virtual or actual, where they go not only for the latest information and techniques but also for advice and for someone to bounce ideas off.

CASE STORY *PSION UK, SIMON'S STORY*

Narrator Simon was customer services manager for this rapidly growing company in the 1990s and was tasked with setting up technical support, customer services and repair functions.

Context The call centre for the PC manufacturer Psion UK was always striving to improve its performance in answering customer phone calls. A quality improvement project was initiated with the objective to improve customer satisfaction levels.

Issue Simon set KPIs that he thought would drive up performance. The main KPI was to answer as many calls in a day as possible and the benchmark was set at 30. The result was, of course, that customer satisfaction went down not up, because agents were getting through the calls as soon as possible and being too curt on the phone.

Solution Simon realised he needed to set relevant and smarter KPIs. He classified calls by type and difficulty and accepted that speed of call answering was not the only indicator of customer satisfaction.

Learning People will respond to what is being measured. If the KPIs are poor, then no matter how well the project is being managed you will not get the end result you require. Spend time translating business needs into measurable project objectives and then think through with key stakeholders what could go wrong. Get as wide as possible buy-in to the objectives before you launch the project.

Getting promoted

It is difficult to specify what you, as a Fast Track project manager, need to do to get promoted, as conditions will change and the criteria for promotion will vary from company to company. In fact very few people now look at a career within a single company and so promotion may mean moving outside a company. Identify whether your company has a 'talent pool' in terms of a recognised high-potential programme for all managers. See how skills and competences in project management could help you get into that talent pool.

Whatever your area of expertise and chosen profession, take time to reflect on your state of readiness for promotion. Identify the future role you are keen to fulfil; clarify the criteria you will need to satisfy in terms of skills, experience, attitudes and behaviours; and consider how you will visibly demonstrate these attributes to others. Ask yourself the following:

→ **Capability**. Do I have what it takes in terms of what I have achieved and learned so far? How can I demonstrate my capabilities in terms of managing projects? (For example, one HR director for a major utility now expects potential project managers to bring in a well-presented portfolio illustrating the projects they have managed or been involved in previously.)

→ **Credibility**. Can I convince others that I can and will perform the role well? Can I get third-party or client testimonies to attest to my skills as a project manager? (This may sound hard to achieve but it is no more than 'personalised marketing', which is an increasing trend in recruiting professionals in the USA.)

→ **Desire**. Do I want the role and do I have sufficient drive and enthusiasm to do a great job? Ask yourself why you want a new role or challenge and then how you would demonstrate this to potential employees – without coming across as desperate.

→ **Relationships**. Do I have positive working relationships with the right people? For internal promotions this is a key factor. Getting along with people may be more important that certain technical skills and competencies, which can be attained later on. Demonstrating your skill at building relationships is the Holy Grail at interviews – according to the HR director of a major UK utility company.

→ **Competitive**. Am I the most appropriate candidate given the internal and external alternatives? Of course you are! Next question.

If you have concerns, then put in place a plan to address them. Timing will be key, so make sure you are well prepared before putting yourself forward for a role.

In terms of increasing your project management responsibility alongside that of your professional role, there is usually a hierarchy within project and portfolio management. In ascending order of complexity and seniority, the roles are often:

→ project manager

→ programme manager (a programme being multiple related projects)

→ project (programme) management office manager

→ project sponsor

→ project director.

Becoming a director

Since the title of this chapter is 'Getting to the top', it seems appropriate to talk about the top role and what you need to aim for. Most large organisations will have a project director or something similar, but few of those we have met have come down the first path we talked about earlier – the so called 'professional' project manager route. Most of them have a separate discipline or expertise in addition to their project management skills and experience – be it new product development, marketing or customer services. In addition, in some organisations the responsibility for managing or overseeing the portfolio of projects at strategic level might be allocated to a specific director, such as the director of marketing, R&D or operations.

Whatever the title, the director in charge of projects or programmes will fulfil various roles in addition to meeting their statutory responsibilities. These include:

→ **Linking projects to business strategy.** This is the so-called strategic project management (SPM) function and requires an understanding of the business strategy but also of the current project capabilities of the business.

→ **Championing projects.** If project management is a discipline central to the success of the business, then ensuring that projects have specific resources and sufficient budgets in the face of internal competition from other areas will be a key responsibility.

→ **Creating a progressive project management environment.** This means ensuring that a culture exists in which projects can be managed professionally and thoroughly. This requires a knowledge of what technology exists to help project managers and what would be appropriate for the business, including the impact of trends in project management (technology) and the impact on the business and projects underway.

→ **Managing the project management office (PMO).** The role here is to get a strategic picture for the board of what projects are underway, the risks involved and the progress to date. Reporting the current projects underway at board level is often a sore point, as unfortunately many boards of directors underestimate the number of projects in progress – some by as much as half.

→ **Managing project resources.** Some organisations devolve project resources to certain departments or disciplines, while some keep them centralised and get departments to bid for the budget and resources in terms of what the projects will deliver. In either scenario, the project director has to track resources against value and results.

In addition to these formal roles, a project director will probably be involved in informally reviewing and auditing project work, as well as mentoring or coaching project managers. These would be useful skills for a new project manager to acquire.

Whatever the style of the project director or the organisation of the business, strategic project management is about three interrelated influences, which are different from those at the lower project management level. Whereas at project management level it is about time, cost and performance, at strategic level it is about strategy, resources and results (see figure).

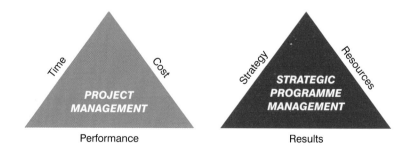

QUICK TIP DEVELOP PERSONAL NETWORKS
As your project management career progresses, build a network of individuals that you can rely on for advice and specialist knowledge.

How do I get to the top?

In project management the 'top' can take many forms. For many people the top lies not within their company as a project director but as an acknowledged expert in an area of project management. They define success as being an expert who is brought in to help companies out when projects are in trouble. Success is being acknowledged as an independent, project troubleshooter.

One reason why people do not associate the role of director of projects with that of being a project 'expert' is because many businesses see project management as an associated *additional* skill which enhances the specific 'trade' skills of managers – such as marketing, operations, finance, etc. So success is achieved by promotion from project manager, through programme manager to a position of seniority within a discipline, i.e. marketing. Project management is thus seen as a means to getting promotion within a discipline, not as a profession in itself.

In fact, for an increasing number of people success in project management is synonymous with independence from full-time employment – meaning you don't have to be employed full-time as an 'expert' project manager to be at the top. It is a skill or discipline that will always be in demand; with a good reputation it is possible to build up a 'portfolio career' gaining project management experience in many different areas, either by joining the company or as a contractor. Many people think that if the situation requires it, a good project manager could step back into full-time employment and use their acquired skills to get back on the career path within a company. Indeed, many businesses are looking at this 'flexible career' mechanism as a means of getting good project managers in when required, but allowing them to get varied experience elsewhere if necessary.

No matter what the 'top' looks like to project managers and directors, many people agree that experience and a good track record in project management, with some degree of formal training, is invaluable. It seems to be that getting to the top in project management nowadays allows individuals a greater degree of flexibility and independence than ever before.

Whatever your definition of success, you should plan ahead. If you want to be a self-employed project manager, then you must understand the needs of your specific target market and skill yourself accordingly. If you wish to stay within your current company and gain promotion, you will have to understand the special needs of your employer and the net-work of contacts required to facilitate your progress through the ranks. In either case, nothing succeeds like successes – a good track record will always be a good starting point for your dreams.

STOP – THINK – ACT

In this final chapter you will have identified what you need to do to get to the top in your chosen career. Your company may not have a project management director or separate project structure, but it is likely that project management is seen as key to the success of the business within the wider operational environment.

As someone skilled in project management you should now take this opportunity to stop and reflect on your career aspirations. Do you want project management to be the core of your future career? If so, then you should be looking towards qualifications and experience in managing projects and membership of the professional project management bodies. However, you might feel that being skilled in project management is simply complementary to your primary discipline, such as marketing or IT. In this case your future direction may lie in following that particular career path. So, stop now and consider – what do you want to be doing in three years' time?

My vision	What do I want to be doing in three years' time?
My supporters	Whose support will I need to get there?
My capabilities	What capabilities and experience will I need to succeed?
My progress	What milestones will I achieve along the way?

Visit **www.Fast-Track-Me.com** to use the Fast Track online planning tool.

Rationality and irrationality in project management

Associate Professor Dirk Pieter van Donk and Dr Eamonn Molloy

Project management know-how has expanded enormously over the past decades. However, numerous studies show that frequent cost overruns, delays and underperformance in terms of quality and user satisfaction seem to have become the rule and the reality of contemporary projects. The response to that has been 'a yet greater emphasis on technology based solutions, quantitative methodologies, positivist methodologies, and a stronger reliance on instrumental rationality'.[1] Such further rationalising of professional project management knowledge is also visible in promoting general usable models and methodologies, like the *Guide to the Project Management Body of Knowledge (PMBOK)*[2] and PRINCE and PRINCE2.[3] In our view this does not help very much in solving the problems faced, nor will it help to generate novel knowledge on project management.

What are the rationalities and irrationalities in current project management?

Projects are often started to change an organisation. Some people state (or advocate) that modern organisations will become networks or project-based entities of loosely coupled projects. The rationality behind opting for project-based organising is that fixed and permanent organisational structures and functional departments are supposed to be no longer capable of dealing with the dynamics and complexities of current organisational environments. However, there seems to be a tension between the standardised project management approaches and the dynamics of organisational change.

Many projects can be seen as being composed of a number of elements that each constitute and are constituted by different technologies. Generally, different parts will be interdependent, and according to project management logic at a certain moment in time these interdependencies have to be fixed and formalised: using the well-known work breakdown structure of project management, key deliverables, etc. However, the more innovative and cutting-edge a part of a project is, the more it will be advantageous to postpone decision making and wait for more innovative solutions and technologies to be available. From the

---

[1] Hodgson, D. and Cicmil, S. (2006), *Making Projects Critical*, London: Palgrave.

[2] Published by the Project Management Institute, third revised edition 2004.

[3] PRojects IN Controlled Environments: a process-based method for effective project management.

EXPERT VOICE

EXPERT VOICE

perspective of that part of the project and the technology, this is entirely rational. However, elsewhere on the project other criteria may have priority and the task of the project management is to choose between competing solutions. Thus there is a misalignment between the speed at which decisions must be taken across different parts of the project.

One of the often acclaimed advantages of project management is that functional silos are broken down. Specifically in large, bureaucratic (government) organisations this might look a rational and sensible argument. A project team consisting of people from different departments and different backgrounds are more likely to come up with the breakthroughs needed for solutions that otherwise would have been blocked by departmental power. This all seems very positive and naïve: a team is supposed to develop its own rationality that breaks the departmental power bases to which team members belong. We rather believe that departments will see the project as an arena to protect their best interests and access to resources, and will correspondingly select and instruct 'their' team members accordingly. This might be seen as the irrationality of power.

Are there scientific solutions for the above problems and what do we need to do to help project managers handling them?

The starting point of our approach is the definition of a project as temporary organisation.[4] The basic element of that definition for us is that projects can be thought of as being organisations. There is a large amount of literature dealing with designing, structuring and managing organisations. Here, we focus on the so-called contingency literature of structuring organisations. The central theoretical point from that literature is that under different circumstances different organisational structures will be needed to be successful and that each organisational structure has its particular coordination and management issues. One of the first to synthesise the research in this field was Henry Mintzberg, in his seminal work *The Structuring of Organizations*.[5]

In a recent paper,[6] we show the relevance of Mintzberg's typology of organisation structures and associated coordination mechanisms for project organisation. The typology helps in detecting the core managerial problems in each form of project organisation. The typology helps (rational) project managers to develop a new perspective on project management theory and the use and misuse of project management instruments and methods.

[4] Lundin, R.A. and Söderhulm, A. (1995), 'A theory of the temporary organization', *Scandinavian Journal of Management*, 11 (4), 437–55.
[5] Mintzberg, H. (1979), *The Structuring of Organizations*, Englewood Cliffs NJ: Prentice-Hall.
[6] Van Donk, D.P. and Molloy, E. (2008), 'From organizing as projects to projects as organizations', *International Journal of Project Management*, 26(2), 129–37.

PART

DIRECTOR'S TOOLKIT

In Part B we introduced ten core tools and techniques that can be used from day one in your new role as a team leader or manager in project management. As you progress up the career ladder to the role of project director, and as your team matures in terms of their understanding and capabilities, you will want to introduce more advanced or sophisticated techniques.

Part D provides a number of essential techniques developed and adopted by industry leaders – helping you to differentiate yourself from your competitors. They are simple and straightforward but their use can radically improve your chances of project success.

	TOOL DESCRIPTION
T1	Team project management audit
T2	Planning techniques
T3	Critical path analysis
T4	Risk management

T1 TEAM PROJECT MANAGEMENT AUDIT

Use the following checklist to assess the current state of your team. Consider each criterion in turn and use the following scoring system to identify current performance:

0 Not done or defined within the business: unaware of its importance to project management

1 Aware of area but little or no work done in the business

2 Recognised as an area of importance and some work done in this area

3 Area clearly defined and work done in terms of project management

4 Consistent use of best practice tools and techniques in this area across the business

5 Area recognised as being 'best in class' and could be a reference for best practice

Reflect on the lowest scores and identify those areas that are critical to success and flag them as status Red, requiring immediate attention. Then identify those areas that you are concerned about and flag those as status Amber, implying areas of risk that need to be monitored closely. Status Green implies that you are happy with the current state.

ID	CATEGORY	EVALUATION CRITERIA	SCORE	STATUS
P1	Business needs		0–5	RAG
A	Align to business imperatives	All current projects are clearly aligned to the business strategy and to strategic priorities	☐	☐
B	Understand consumer requirements	All projects reflect customer and consumer needs within their objectives and supporting information, be they internal or external	☐	☐
C	Identify links to other projects	The interdependencies between projects are highlighted in the projects' charter, from either a risk management or synergies perspective	☐	☐
P2	Project goals			
A	Set objectives	All projects have clearly understood, actionable SMART objectives	☐	☐
B	Agree key performance indicators	All projects have clear and agreed KPIs and return on investment (ROI) targets	☐	☐
C	Establish the business case	The organisation understands how important each project is to delivering value to the business and the business case has been agreed by all stakeholders	☐	☐
P3	Stakeholders			
A	Identify stakeholders	Project managers and their core teams understand the key stakeholders and have carried out some stakeholder analysis	☐	☐
B	Assess commitment	The commitment of project stakeholders has been assessed and the core project team is aware of the results	☐	☐
C	Influence supporters and resisters	A communication plan has been created to address the commitment, or otherwise, of project supporters or resisters	☐	☐

ID	CATEGORY	EVALUATION CRITERIA	SCORE	STATUS
P4	Workplan and timings		0–5	RAG
A	Define tasks and priorities	All projects have a list of defined and identified tasks and the structure of the project is clear	☐	☐
B	Identify critical path	The critical path has been calculated and the earliest finish date of the project is understood	☐	☐
C	Agree milestones	Milestones against which progress will be checked have been set appropriately	☐	☐
P5	Issues and risks			
A	Identify issues and risks	A risk register or log has been opened and is used throughout projects. Risks are reviewed and prioritised at team meetings	☐	☐
B	Agree corrective actions	Actions to address risks are identified and plans changed accordingly	☐	☐
C	Manage change requests	A change management process is in place for all projects and changes to the scope and plan of the project are managed by the project manager at regular meetings	☐	☐
P6	The team			
A	Select project leader	The project manager (leader) has content and process experience relevant to the project in hand	☐	☐
B	Build the team	The team has a balance of skills, which complement those of the project manager. The team has a common agreed goal	☐	☐
C	Agree roles and responsibilities	The roles and responsibilities of the core project team are clear and understood by all	☐	☐
P7	Critical decisions			
A	Identify decisions	All decisions and their reasons are recorded for audit purposes	☐	☐
B	Agree decision-making process	The process by which issues are decided upon in the project is understood and authority levels are agreed	☐	☐
C	Gain buy-in	All stakeholders are informed of major changes in the project (scope or plan) and their input is sought and potential conflicts addressed	☐	☐

ID	CATEGORY	EVALUATION CRITERIA	SCORE	STATUS
P8	**Resources and budget**		0–5	RAG
A	Identify resource requirements	Resources (consumables, materials, skills, etc.) are identified up front	☐	☐
B	Specify quantity and quality	All resources identified have clear quantitative and qualitative standards attached	☐	☐
C	Agree budgets	All project budgets are understood and total up-front project funding is agreed with the project sponsor and/or finance director	☐	☐
P9	**Project leadership**			
A	Right skills	The project manager and project sponsor have the right process and content skills and complement each other	☐	☐
B	Right thinking	The project manager understands not only the process of delivering a project but also the bigger picture and where the project fits, in order to be able to make the right decisions when appropriate	☐	☐
C	Right commitment	The project manager and sponsor are committed to the successful delivery of the project and its business outcomes, despite any personal reservations	☐	☐
P10	**Communications**			
A	Upward	A process and platform exists for communicating progress and escalating issues to the business, the project review board (PRB), the project sponsor and/or customers	☐	☐
B	Sideways	A process and platform exists for communicating project and resource issues to other project managers and functional heads	☐	☐
C	Downwards	A process and platform exists for communicating with the project team, suppliers and/or project specialists as necessary	☐	☐

For each element of the checklist add up the scores of the three related questions and divide by three – this will give you an average score for that specific element. Here is an example:

ELEMENT	SCORE	0	1	2	3	4	5	NOTES
Business needs	2			■				Limited link to strategy
Project goals	4					■		
Stakeholders	2.6			■				Some stakeholder analysis
Workplan and timings	4					■		
Issues and risks	1		■					Limited risk management
The team	3				■			Average team building
Critical decisions	2			■				Poor decision making
Resources and budget	5						■	
Project leadership	1		■					Limited leadership skills
Communications	2.5			■				Poor communication process

In an integrated project management framework the whole system is only as good as an individual element. If one link in the chain is weak then the framework within the company will not operate to optimum efficiency and there is increased risk of failure. The action plan, therefore, should be to focus attention and resources on the elements of greatest weakness first, and then to move the whole framework to a level of excellence. This approach optimises the use of resources and sets up a process of continuous improvement.

In the example above, the managers conducting a review have identified that the weakest links are those in the areas of risk management (*issues and risks*) and *project leadership* (average scores 1). The plan would therefore be to focus attention on and improve risk management as a discipline within projects and to assess where and how project leadership could be improved. Once the senior management team has increased confidence that risk management and project leadership have improved, the next stage would be to focus on areas in Amber (*business needs*, *critical decisions* and *communications* – average scores 2–2.5).

T2 PLANNING TECHNIQUES

How do you structure your overall project plan? What tools and techniques are there to help the Fast Track manager lay out their project tasks in such a way as to make planning easier and more straightforward and to facilitate the total project planning process?

In this toolkit we offer three distinct tools and techniques that can be used by the Fast Track project manager in most projects. The key is to use them first on a simple and straightforward project, and then as projects increase in size and complexity you will find that these tools will help you more and more. The three planning techniques are the work breakdown structure (WBS), the Gantt chart and the stage and gate phase-based approach.

The work breakdown structure (WBS)

The WBS is a core planning tool, whose benefits are often not realised by those new to project management. In its simplest form it is a collection of tasks that add up to the completed project – a breakdown of work to be done, hence 'work breakdown structure'.

There are two basic forms: the indented list format and the organisation chart format. Which you use is a matter of personal preference; however, the indented list format works well with software and allows further in-depth planning when using a spreadsheet. The two formats are shown below: you will see that the numbers represent the same deliverables and tasks but are laid out differently.

Indented list format

1.0 Materials created

1.1 Format agreed

1.2 Research completed

1.3 Forms printed

2.0 Venue organised

2.1 Venue booked

2.1.1 Facilities checked

2.1.2 Site visited

2.2 Transport organised

3.0 Conference held

Organisation chart format

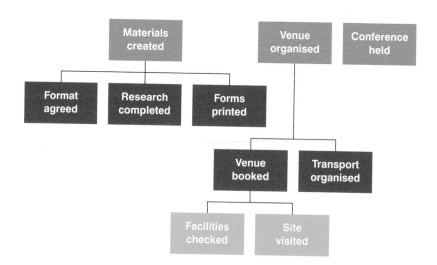

Common errors

Despite the simplicity of this tool many people make some basic errors when using work breakdown structures in either format:

→ **Tasks not headings.** The tasks represented by the numbers in the example above are exactly that – tasks. They are *not* headings under which you collate jobs. The high-level 'deliverables' as they are known, represented by the blue elements, should, in a project, be written as tasks. For example 'software written' or 'materials ordered' are examples of good clear and concise tasks. Where people tend to go wrong is they use these as headings and state them as 'software' or 'materials'. This leads to confusion because it underestimates what actually has to be done. What does 'software' or 'materials' actually mean in a project context? Instead, use a brief statement with a verb in it. The WBS is about action, so it should have an 'action word' in it.

→ **High-level versus detailed planning.** The best way to create a comprehensive WBS is to get the high-level tasks right *first*. These dictate the structure or style of the project. Only then, when you are happy with the high-level structure, do you break the elements down into detail. This is a great team-building exercise and gets everyone involved in the structure of the project. As a Fast Track project manager you might want to dictate the high-level tasks and style of project layout and then get the project members to create the detail. However, beware of jumping into a meticulous level of detail straight away. Do not underestimate the power of the humble Post-it note at this stage of the planning process. Such a low-tech tool is great for getting teams to understand the structure and detail of the project. Get the core project team in a room (with a big blank wall) and ask them to write all the high-level tasks on the Post-it notes. Once these have been posted on the wall, ask them to break the tasks into detail. As a Fast Track project manager you might want to transcribe all the Post-it notes on to your PC before the notes start to fall off the wall. Use software tools like Vision or Microsoft Excel to capture the structure and detail of the Post-it notes on your PC.

→ **Too much detail.** Precisely because the WBS is the most useful tool for laying out what has to be done, many people who are new to project management use the WBS 'to death'. The key question is: 'How much detail is enough?' There is no right or wrong answer to this and many techniques can be used, relating to things like the complexity or duration of the project or the individual value of resources. As a general rule we would recommend that you break down the tasks to the level of detail at which the resource (person or team) doing the work actually knows what to do and to what quality standard. If you break down the work into greater and greater detail, you cross the line between telling a person *what* to do and telling them *how* to do it. This has major disadvantages: it is demotivating for the individual, assumes that you know best in all things and creates too many detailed tasks that you, as a project manager, will have to check up on. Getting the level of detail right does depend upon you knowing the skills and expertise of your staff and those involved in the project tasks – so get out and talk to your project members. An effective project manager is not one who sits behind a PC and blindly issues tasks for 'resources' to deliver. Understanding the level of competence of those people doing the tasks will greatly influence the level of planning you require and make your life as a Fast Track project manager so much easier.

→ **Duplication.** A common risk of creating a project WBS using Post-it notes and separate teams is the duplication of tasks. As a Fast Track project manager, one of your key roles in the planning stage is to ensure that similar or same tasks are not called different things and appear in different parts of the WBS. Ask for a clear explanation of the tasks and see whether they are duplicated elsewhere in the plan. Ask if they can be merged and therefore efficiencies made.

Remember that when you are happy with the style, detail and content of the WBS, it is still possible for your project teams to break it down further for their own requirements. Software such as Microsoft Project and Excel allows you to 'zip' up or down the detail of the WBS as appropriate, but remember that you need a master WBS to use as your basis for planning and management of the project.

The Gantt chart

Linking seamlessly into the WBS is the best graphic available in project management – the Gantt chart (invented by Henry Gantt, engineer and consultant). Available in many formats and variations, this is the single most useful diagram for project managers and project team members. At its most basic, it simply shows WBS tasks against a timeline, where the duration of a task is shown as a bar or line. A basic example is shown below:

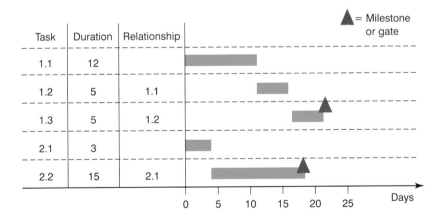

The timeline on the bottom axis can be actual dates or just days (as above) and the side axis can have detail such as the WBS number, task name, duration and (as above) the relationship or dependency between tasks. Make sure you understand what you can put into your Gantt chart and what people actually need to see. With modern project management software you can create highly complex Gantt charts, but you can also create very simple ones by just using a spreadsheet.

Common errors

→ **Too much information.** Keep your Gantt charts simple at first. Understand the needs of those people wanting project information and what the Gantt chart can supply. As you get more experienced, you will discover what else you can add to your Gantt chart and you will be tempted to add more and more detail. Keep in mind the needs of those people you are communicating with at all times. Use the Gantt chart as a learning tool for yourself, so every time you create a new Gantt chart, see what else you could add, while considering the needs of your project team. A Gantt chart should be easy to read and understand and require minimal explanation.

→ **Version control.** Make sure that you are all singing from the same hymn sheet! When you create a new Gantt chart for the project, always put a version number or date on it, as otherwise you are creating a major problem for yourself when dealing with remote teams. With modern IT systems and project software you can ensure that there is a master version and that only a few people have editor-access to change the Gantt chart. The software should also make sure that every new version has a new version number or creation date. If you are simply creating Gantt charts for the first time using a spreadsheet or crayons and paper then *do remember* to add a date or version number.

→ **Printing out.** Even with the most advanced project management software, when you try to print out the Gantt chart on to paper there may be problems. Many a time we have entered a project manager's office only to find them on their knees sticking various A4 sheets together to create a comprehensive Gantt chart for all to see. Alternatively the font size is reduced so that all tasks can be fitted on to as few sheets as possible – but the problem then is that you need a magnifying glass to read the chart. Even if you have access to a plotting machine (large-scale printer), remember that as soon as you print out your Gantt on to paper it will be out of date. So in all cases ask yourself who the Gantt chart is for and why you are printing it out. Think how long it will remain current and whether you could print out a 'personalised' reduced-level Gantt chart instead of the whole thing.

The Gantt chart is invaluable as a tool, but you need to learn how to make it work for you and get to know its intricacies and complexities as you develop as a Fast Track project manager.

Stage and gate planning

A stage and gate process is a way of laying out your workplan and checking progress or objectives along the way. 'Stage' reflects the part of a project where work is done and 'gate' reflects a point at which progress is reviewed or objectives checked.

The table below reflects the generic tasks that could be included in each stage of a project. Not all will be applicable to all projects, and many will need to be adapted to suit your business and your specific project needs. The lists are fairly comprehensive and as such look a little daunting. Go through them and decide where you need to take a shortcut or adapt the methodology to take account of your specific case and timescale constraints. Sometimes you have to go for it and leave a few stones unturned.

Reflect on each item and assess a current project you are working on. Assess each activity using a simple RAG scale for status, where Red suggests major concerns and that you should take immediate corrective actions, Amber suggests some concerns and risks, and needs to be monitored closely, and Green indicates useful activity that is on track.

WORKPLAN		DESCRIPTION OF POSSIBLE ACTIVITIES	STATUS
Stage 1 Initiate			
1	Strategic priorities	Review strategic, product-market and brand imperatives to identify project scope, direction and product/market/process priorities	☐
2	Market analysis	Conduct analysis to understand macro-economic trends, current and prospective customers, end-users/consumers and key competitors. Research best practices and market leaders	☐

WORKPLAN	DESCRIPTION OF POSSIBLE ACTIVITIES	STATUS
Stage 1 Initiate (contd)		
3 Internal audit	Conduct an internal audit of core capabilities (all aspects of the supply chain) and summarise in the form of critical strengths and weaknesses	☐
4 Initial idea review (concept)	Review the databases of previous similar project ideas, case studies and possible failed projects. Get buy-in for concept review at high level. Conduct stakeholder analysis. Assess scope of project: cost reduction, product development, customer expansion or new product development?	☐
5 Initial idea review (concept+)	Develop idea in more detail, including financial viability assessment at +/– 20% accuracy. Conduct high-level risk management informally. Gain key stakeholder support	☐
6 Project charter	Initiate the formal project charter, including outline idea, outline profit and loss (P&L), potential project leader and in-market period	☐
7 Preliminary screen	Conduct a preliminary formal financial and capability screening and risk assessment. Use 'quick screening' criteria, including assessment against value contribution, strategic/brand fit, stakeholder acceptance, implementation feasibility and timescales (V-SAFE)	☐
8 Timing and dependencies	Identify preliminary timings and intra-project dependencies and explore potential critical issues/resources	☐
10 Idea approval **Gate 1**	Complete formal idea evaluation (Go, No Go/Kill, Modify or Wait) and prepare gate documents	☐
Stage 2 Business case		
1 Team initiation	Assign project leader(s) and initial members of the core team. Conduct project team kick-off workshop. Identify training needs and develop capability plans where necessary	☐
2 Concept development	Develop top-level concept (draft) and develop core project idea. Test the concept (conduct qualitative analysis – brand positioning and target audience). Refine the concept based on test results	☐
3 Brief	Develop product or solution brief with opportunity assessment. Gain feedback from relevant functions (financial, sales and marketing, R&D, quality assurance, operations, trading, legal, market research, etc.)	☐

WORKPLAN	DESCRIPTION OF POSSIBLE ACTIVITIES	STATUS

Stage 2 Business (contd)

4	Proof of concept	Pre-prototype and conduct qualitative consumer tests (if appropriate), including user/consumer validation	☐
5	Operational impact	Conduct preliminary assessment of impact on manufacturing, operations and supply chain/route to market	☐
6	Initial financials	Agree preliminary sales/financial forecasts, market share and value (price, cost and investments), and create a multi-year forecast and preliminary return on investment (including assumptions). Include portfolio assessment and potential synergy with other projects and programmes	☐
7	Stakeholder buy-in	Gain formal stakeholder agreement to the business case, capital expenditure (CapEx), go-live activities, route to market, manufacturing and legal/claims	☐
8	Project plans	Agree initial project timetable. Develop a communication strategy/plan. Construct Gantt chart in various stages of detail	☐
9	Risk assessment	Conduct formal risk assessment on project plan, assumptions and capabilities	☐
10	Project financials	Develop preliminary P&L forecast with return on investment (ROI) and financial payback	☐
11	Business case approval **Gate 2**	Finalise business case and prepare gate documents for presentation	☐

Stage 3 Develop

1	Prototype development	Create a project solution prototype and validate internally. Conduct user/consumer tests (quantitative) or pilot test prototype (as appropriate)	☐
2	Product refinement	Fine-tune the project solution based on user/consumer feedback (product, package, positioning, pricing, etc.) and modify as required. Conduct technical tests (and field trials if required)	☐
3	Regulatory and trademark	Gain quality, compliance, regulatory, trademark and legal clearance (internal/external)	☐
4	Final specification	Develop final project solution specification and agree with key stakeholders and relevant elements of the supply chain	☐
5	Product briefs	Develop an outline communication plan based on agreed positioning and sensitivities. Develop an internal PR plan and internal sell-in pack	☐

WORKPLAN	DESCRIPTION OF POSSIBLE ACTIVITIES	STATUS
Stage 3 Develop (contd)		
6 Stakeholder commitment	Gain stakeholder agreement to final business case and launch plan and commitment to implementation support	☐
7 Launch plan	Develop financial plan with three-year P&L forecast, develop preliminary go-live plan and communication strategy, confirm required investments	☐
8 Final business case **Gate 3**	Finalise project budgets and timetable, and prepare gate documents	☐
Stage 4 Implement		
1 'Go' authorisation **Gate 4**	Obtain formal authorisations/sign-offs as required (capital, product, governance and legal/regulatory)	☐
2 Supply chain changes	Implement supply chain/logistics changes and develop production and distribution capability as required	☐
3 Marketing materials	Finalise internal and external marketing materials. Develop sales material and produce samples for sales preparation. Develop advertising material and incentives and purchase media as required	☐
4 Communication plan	Develop communication plan – what (key messages) to whom (stakeholders). Confirm key stakeholder support and clarify deliverables. Develop 'selling story' and develop support materials around the core idea	☐
5 Media strategy	Complete a detailed media strategy with question and answers (Q&As), statements and press releases, including stories, reference sells and claims	☐
6 Sales presentations	Conduct sales presentations and modify materials based on initial feedback	☐
7 Pilot launch	Conduct a limited scope commercial launch to test all aspects of the project and supply chain	☐
8 Success indicators	Identify and agree key success factors (KSFs), key performance indicators (KPIs) (initial and ongoing) and success hurdles. Conduct formal review of end point. Update risk assessment	☐
9 Growth options	Create options and plans for ongoing user/customer support, internal solution life-cycle management and future expansion as required	☐

WORKPLAN	DESCRIPTION OF POSSIBLE ACTIVITIES	STATUS
Stage 4 Implement (contd)		
10 Manage change of scope	Monitor launch plan (completion of tasks), identify and resolve (or escalate) critical issues and risks, motivate the team (identify additional development needs) and conduct regular review meetings	☐
Stage 5 Close and review		
1 Assessment of tasks	Conduct formal review of all work and deliverables to assess completion	☐
2 Sales and marketing	Execute communication plan and activate media launch	☐
3 Early indicators	Conduct performance audits, track performance in market (specifically early indicators) and adjust plans as required	☐
4 Performance reviews **Gate 5**	Review performance against success indicators (KPIs) – did the project deliver on time and within budget and what needs to change for next time?	☐
5 Stakeholder reviews	Conduct formal close-down reviews (meetings) with key stakeholders, including user/customer/ consumer groups and supply chain	☐
6 Team congratulations	Congratulate and disband the team, update personal development plans (PDPs) and agree next roles	☐
7 Lessons learned	Capture and share learning and insights with other teams, update 'best practice' databases and communicate to interested parties	☐
8 Operational handover **Gate 6**	Formally transfer ownership and responsibility to operational teams. Scale operations as required or exit/close	☐

T3 CRITICAL PATH ANALYSIS

Critical path analysis is a crucial technique for those project managers looking to identify means by which they can shorten the duration of their project – sometimes called 'crunching the project plan'. It can be a complicated technique to understand but – as with most tools and techniques – there is an essence of simplicity at its core. Understanding what the critical path is and how to calculate it can give you a real advantage as a Fast Track project manager, yet we are astounded by the number of people who either don't know how to calculate it or don't know what it can do for them.

The basic premise of the critical path is that not all activities in your project will have to start at the same time in order to meet the project's planned completion date. Put all the activities into a logical sequence or order. Estimate the duration of each task and then devise a project schedule. Once you have done that, you can start to see where there are areas that can be 'crunched'. Follow this simple process:

1 **Estimate timings.** Crucial to an effective schedule is accurate timings. If you do not know how long it will take to do something, then look for guidance and help from other managers who may have done something similar before. Their experience is crucial, as getting wildly wrong estimates at this planning stage will cause real problems later on. Make sure you have your team members involved at this stage as they might have more accurate ideas of duration for certain tasks. If in doubt, get best- and worst-case estimates and use your gut feel to create a compromise.

2 **Create a network diagram.** A network diagram shows the relationship between activities and which tasks depend on the completion of other tasks. The diagram will be simple or complex, depending upon how many activities there are and their interrelationship. The Post-it note can be useful here because you can write a separate activity on each note and then lay out the notes in a logical sequence. A simple network diagram is shown below.

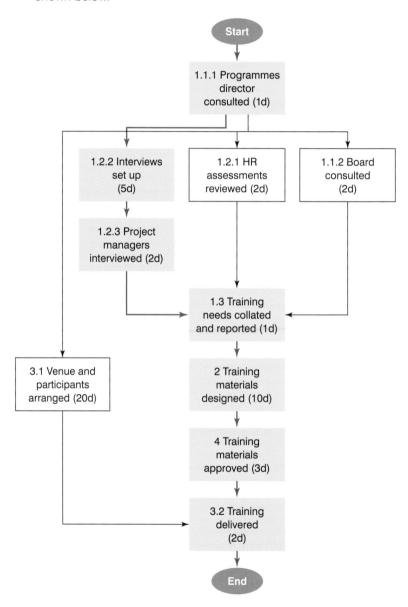

3 **Estimate total time.** When you have created a network diagram you will probably have several 'paths' or routes from start to finish. In the example above, after task 1.1.1 the network splits into four differing paths. Use the duration estimates for each individual task to make a total path estimate by adding them up. The longest route is known as the critical path and shows the shortest possible duration for the project. In the network diagram above, the critical path is highlighted in red and the total project duration from critical path calculation is 24 days (24d).

So what?

What does the critical path do for the Fast Track project manager? Once you have calculated the critical path in your project you can:

→ **Know the total duration of your project.** Understanding this means that you can plan resources accordingly and understand how much you need to shorten your project plan to achieve your planned end date ('crunching the plan').

→ **Understand the risks of slippage.** If a task on the critical path slips by a week, then the whole project will slip by a week. Project planners use critical path analysis to identify these crucial risks and scenarios.

→ **Understand how much 'slack' tasks may have.** Tasks not on the critical path may have what is known as 'slack time'. Basically they have a 'window' by which they should be completed and therefore by understanding this you can plan flexibly. However, if these tasks exceed this slack period they will become part of the critical path and any further delay will delay the whole project.

→ **Decide where to put extra resources.** If you want to speed up your project and 'crunch' the project plan, where do you put those extra resources to reduce duration? On the tasks in the critical path, of course. By reducing their individual duration, you will reduce the overall project. However, note that you will only reduce the overall project duration to the point at which the next longest path through your network diagram becomes the longest critical path.

→ **Prioritise your diary.** Since as the project manager you are undoubtedly the most important person in the project, and since you know that tasks on the critical path are critical, then critical path analysis will give you a subtle hint as to where you should be as a manager to supervise the performance of tasks.

→ **Identify bottlenecks or resource limitations.** The critical path will identify choke points in your project, where it becomes crucial to risk-manage the resources available. Look at your network diagram and see where various multiple paths all go through a single task. That is a bottleneck and you need to plan accordingly to ensure that that task goes to plan.

→ **Communicate your plans.** By explaining to the project team, stakeholders and resource owners what your critical path is they can help you with planning and resource conflicts. You may have to explain what the critical path concept is to some people, but once they understand its importance – to you as the project manager and to them in terms of emphasis and priorities of tasks – they may perform that little bit better.

The critical path is one of the few tools and techniques that we suggest you, as a Fast Track project manager, should get under your belt and learn to use as much as possible. Without this technique you will never be truly confident about shortening the duration of your projects or becoming efficient and effective with resources.

As external project managers we are often involved in projects that have got into difficulties with clients. We ask for three things at the very start of the work we do with clients:

→ **Who is the key stakeholder?** We want to know who can kill off a project and who is really interested in supporting the project we're going to get involved with.

→ **What are the stated objectives?** Without knowing what success looks like, then no matter how good we are as project managers or consultants we are never going to 'win'.

→ **What is the project's critical path?** Without this, we are going to have real difficulties in getting the project back on track and 'crunching' the project plan. If the client asks, 'What's the critical path?' we seriously ask ourselves whether they know how much difficulty the project has got into and whether the project is salvageable at all. The critical path is a crucial piece of project management information – without which project management becomes increasingly risky.

T4 RISK MANAGEMENT

Even with the best planned projects something will go wrong. Unexpected events can throw a project off course and threaten an important objective. If you identify critical risks in advance and assess their significance to the success of the project, you can start to plan accordingly.

Identify risks

Brainstorm with your project team to identify the risks that could threaten or delay the whole project. You need to be focused at this point or these sessions could rapidly turn into cloud-gazing with no real benefit. Try to be as specific as possible in identifying these areas of concern. Taking a look at the tasks and parts of the project that are on the critical path is a good starting point. Beware comments like these:

→ 'We've never done this before.' In this case the task is an ideal candidate for some risk management. If you've never done this task before, you won't see the problems until they hit you. Think out the risks beforehand.

→ 'This always goes wrong!' So might it be a good idea to work out why and put some preventive measures in to stop it going wrong again?

→ 'This is the expensive bit, I hope it doesn't go wrong!' Murphy's Law will apply here – 'anything that can go wrong will', so it's probably no use trusting to hope but instead you need to plan for risks accordingly.

Look also for assumptions in your plan and areas where you are not really sure how things will pan out so you just hope for the best.

Potential problems

Once you've identified these areas of concern, start thinking about what could go wrong. Be specific, detailed and precise, as this will help you later on in planning actions. Draw up a list, which will be your 'risk register'. Review this regularly, especially when you are possibly changing the scope or direction of your project. For each potential problem, assess the probability and impact of each threat. This is because risk, as a concept, is made up of two distinct parts – the chance of something happening (risk or probability) and the impact of it (result or effect).

You don't need to go into huge areas of detail when assessing probability or impact. A simple High, Medium and Low or 1–10 rating will suffice. By assessing the probability and impact of a potential problem you are prioritising management time and effort on those high risks. Your risk register can be as simple or as complicated as you wish to make it, but a simple table like the one below should suffice for most small-scale projects.

ACTIVITY GROUP	IDENTIFY THE GROUP THAT WILL BE AFFECTED BY THE RISK
Risk	What is the risk? What might occur that would affect the activity group?
Probability that the risk will occur	High, Medium or Low?
Impact on project objectives	High, Medium or Low?

Identify likely causes

To plan effective actions, you now need to identify the likely causes of the top potential problems. For each potential problem, identify what you think the likely cause could be. Try to be as specific as possible, as at this point it is very easy for risk management to mushroom out of control with lots of ideas – some relevant, some not so. You might even try to group the likely causes to give you an understanding of where the risks originate. So for each potential problem, identify the likely causes and for each of these likely causes rate their probability – High, Medium or Low. At this stage we are really asking ourselves, 'How likely is likely?' A table might help, like the one below.

POTENTIAL PROBLEM	IDENTIFY THE GROUP THAT WILL BE AFFECTED BY THE RISK (SEE ABOVE TABLE)
Likely causes	What is the likely cause of this problem? What else?
Group of cause	Is the cause technical, training, human, planning, etc.?
Likelihood	High, Medium or Low?

Action planning

Risk management is all about action. Many times people go through an effective risk management process but forget that at the end of the risk assessment you actually have to do something. There are two distinct sets of actions that you can take as a project manager and each affects risks in a different way:

→ **Preventive actions.** Also known as proactive actions, their focus is to 'prevent' or make less likely a cause. They need to be planned in advance and then the project plan needs to be changed accordingly. These actions require a change of the project plan at some point, and as a result a decision needs to be made as to the amount of change, the budget for the change, the effect on the project and objectives, and who is going to carry out these actions.

→ **Mitigating actions.** Also known as contingent actions, Plan B or reactive actions, their purpose is to reduce the effects of the potential problem when it has occurred. They need to be planned in advance and invested in, but they may never actually be used at all. If the problem doesn't occur, then they will not be required. In terms of project planning, you need to set aside time to create these contingency plans and put them into your risk register.

Review risks regularly

Maintaining an overview of the risks that might threaten your project is critical to the project's success or failure. You will need to establish a simple system that will make it immediately apparent where the high risks are and when they have happened – a 'trigger'.

The major problem or 'risk' with risk management is that the team gets involved in planning risks for everything and therefore overplans. This sucks up management time and has little discernable benefit to the project. We recommend that you allocate time at regular meetings to review the risk register and focus only on those risks that are Red. These are the risks that pose the greatest danger to the project's objectives. The easiest way to assess them is to use the matrix below.

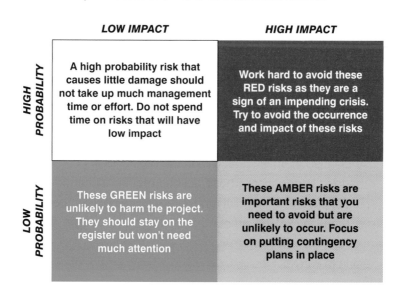

	LOW IMPACT	**HIGH IMPACT**
HIGH PROBABILITY	A high probability risk that causes little damage should not take up much management time or effort. Do not spend time on risks that will have low impact	Work hard to avoid these RED risks as they are a sign of an impending crisis. Try to avoid the occurrence and impact of these risks
LOW PROBABILITY	These GREEN risks are unlikely to harm the project. They should stay on the register but won't need much attention	These AMBER risks are important risks that you need to avoid but are unlikely to occur. Focus on putting contingency plans in place

THE FAST TRACK WAY

Take time to reflect

Within the Fast Track series, we cover a lot of ground quickly. Depending on your current role, company or situation, some ideas will be more relevant than others. Go back to your individual and team audits and reflect on the 'gaps' you have identified, and then take time to review each of the top ten tools and techniques and list of technologies.

Next steps

Based on this review, you will identify many ideas about how to improve your performance, but look before you leap: take time to plan your next steps carefully. Rushing into action is rarely the best way to progress unless you are facing a crisis. Think carefully about your own personal career development and that of your team. Identify a starting place and consider what would have a significant impact on performance and be easy to implement. Then make a simple to-do list with timings for completion.

Staying ahead

Finally, the fact that you have taken time to read and think hard about the ideas presented here suggests that you are already a professional in your chosen discipline. However, all areas of business leadership are changing rapidly and you need to take steps to stay ahead as a leader in your field. Take time to log in to the Fast Track web-resource, at **www.Fast-Track-Me.com**, and join a community of like-minded professionals.

Good luck!

OTHER TITLES IN THE FAST TRACK SERIES

This title is one of many in the Fast Track series that you may be interested in exploring. Whilst each title works as a standalone solution, together they provide a comprehensive cross-functional approach that creates a common business language and structure. The series includes titles on the following:

→ Strategy

→ Innovation

→ Finance

→ Sales

→ Marketing

GLOSSARY

agile A project management methodology initially developed for software development projects which uses an iterative approach to refining and redeveloping deliverables

analysis paralysis The process by which too many people are asked for their input and opinion too early in the project initiation phase and as a result the project manager or sponsor is overloaded with contradictory opinions and advice. Although buy-in and communication are good, sometimes you have to make the decision yourself

business case A document illustrating the business (economic) reasons for the project, rather than the technical reasons. Sometimes incorporated into the project charter

change Dealing with change within a project is the major skill required of a project manager. Changes will occur irrespective of how much planning has been done. Using issue and change logs and having a change control process will help here

change control A general term describing the procedures used in a project to ensure that changes are introduced in a controlled and coordinated manner. For example, it could include the control of different versions of documents and charts as a project progresses, to ensure all involved in a project are working from the most up-to-date information

change request A formal process by which an individual requests that the scope of a project be changed. This requires consent (often by the PRB) and will usually involve extra cost.

Control of change requests helps keep projects on track and within budget

close-down The formal part of a project where the project is finished. After this point a costing process can be completed to assess the full true costs of the project. A review of the project may happen after the close-down, to assess how a project actually went, but this review is often not included in project costs

close-down checklist Much of the value of a project is lost on closure. A simple checklist to validate whether a project was a total success is very useful to an organisation. It should contribute to a lessons-learned knowledge database

communication plan A plan by which all stakeholders are informed of project progress and issues. Created by the project manager, its aim is to keep stakeholders informed and therefore committed, right through to the formal project review

contingency funding Funding and/or resources released for use only when specific criteria have been met. It is usually used when a project overruns or a specific risk has to be mitigated through the use of contingency plans – it should not be used as a general 'cushion' for poor planning

contingency plan 'Plan B' – the output of a formal risk assessment within a project. A contingency plan helps to minimise the effect of a problem on a project or part of a project. It is implemented once a project trigger has been tripped. It may be small and change the project scope slightly, or it could completely change the project

creativity The process of generating and thinking about new ideas. This is often difficult to insert into project management as a discipline, especially when the project is underway

critical path analysis (CPA) A formula for scheduling a set of project activities. It is a very important tool for effective project management. CPA calculates the longest path of planned activities to the end of the project, and the earliest and latest date that each activity can start and finish without making the project longer. This process determines which activities are 'critical'. The critical path is the sequence of project network activities that add up to the longest overall duration. This determines the shortest time possible to complete the project

dependency The link between two or more activities within a project ('task dependency')

duration The time it takes from the start to the finish of a deliverable or task. Duration should *not* be confused with task time or effort

earned value management (EVM) A technique used for measuring project progress in an objective manner. EVM compares technical performance, schedule performance and cost performance

estimation The calculation and approximation of results based upon incomplete data. In project management, it is often used in planning phases to set schedules, deadlines, resource use and costs

feasibility study A short, preliminary study undertaken to assess the viability and validity of a full-scale project

float Often known as 'slack', it is the amount of time that a task in a project network can be delayed

without causing a delay either to the end of the project or to subsequent tasks. It is best thought of as 'spare' time or a 'window of opportunity'

Gantt chart A plan of activities within a project presented graphically as a series of boxes against a timeline (a bar chart on its side). The technique was developed by Henry Gantt as a highly effective way of communicating plans and progress to stakeholders

insights Practical tips and techniques gleaned from a formal and semi-formal review of the project at the close-down stage. They are generally categorised as process insights (i.e. 'How could we do this better next time?') and content insights (i.e. 'Was the result what we wanted?').

issue log A continually updated log outlining deviations from project scope or issues that need to be addressed to keep the project on track. It can be very complex, since issues can be prioritised, categorised or addressed in many different ways

kick-off meetings Ideally the implementation phase of a project should start with a formal kick-off meeting at which the objectives are reviewed and plans confirmed. Face-to-face meetings are best, although tele and video conferences can also help. Kick-off meetings are a chance for the project leader to inspire and motivate

meetings A necessary evil required to manage projects. People run projects, not software, so it is important that meetings are planned in advance and are managed effectively. They should focus on the past ('What have we done?'), the present ('Where are we now? Are we on track? What are the issues?') and the future ('What is coming up? What are the risks?')

milestone An event that marks a significant point within the project schedule. In theory it can be at any time, but in practice milestones are usually installed at the beginning or end of a series of tasks, phases or sub-projects. A milestone in itself consumes no resources, effort or time, but is simply a point at which to reference progress against plan

phased-based approach A methodology used to plan and manage projects. Classically, four phases have been used: initiation, planning (design), implementation (execution) and close and review. Organisations should seek to create a phased-based methodology that best suits their organisation and projects

PRINCE2 A project management methodology, in which the intellectual property belongs to the Office of Government Commerce (OGC). It is quite a heavyweight process that is useful for certain types of project only

programme management The management of multiple (related) projects by a programme manager

project A series of activities designed to deliver a goal, with an agreed start and end point. What constitutes a project is often hotly debated, but most discrete activities within an organisation can be defined as projects

project alignment The concept where projects should be directly linked to business needs and contribute to the business objectives. If there is no alignment to business imperatives, then the validity of the whole project should be questioned

project budget The costs associated with the delivery of the project to the agreed standard within known constraints. The budget should include some contingency funding

project charter Sometimes called 'project definition', at its most basic it is a statement of the scope, objectives and participants of a project. However, it can get more detailed and complex and include other elements such as stakeholder benefits and 'negative' objectives or constraints

project communications plan Linked to the concept of stakeholder management, the project communications plan is an approach to managing how people involved in or affected by the project are communicated with: the timings, means of communication, etc.

project diary A technique in which all meetings are planned in advance and the individual diaries of key team members are collated. This helps with the planning of meetings and stakeholder management. It should not to be confused with the project's master schedule

project initiation document (PID) The purpose of a PID is to bring together the key information needed to start the project properly and to convey that information to all concerned with the project. In short, this is the 'who, why, what, when and how' part of the project

project leadership As distinct from (technical) project management, project leadership requires the ability to motivate and inspire those involved in the project and to bring stakeholders on board. Project managers should strive to be project leaders

project management The process of defining, planning, managing and controlling project activities. This will include the monitoring of performance improvement targets and the selection and motivation of the team

Project Management Body of Knowledge (PMBOK) An internationally recognised standard from the Project Management Institute (PMI) that provides the fundamentals of project management as they apply to a wide range of projects. It contains 44 processes in five groups and nine knowledge areas

project management office (PMO) A function, usually within larger companies, that oversees and assists initial project planning. It may also support the project manager with the timely submission of project reports, to a certain standard or template, and work towards solving inter-project conflicts

project management triangle The typical constraints affecting the management of a project: time, cost and project scope. A change in any one factor will have an effect on the other two, to some degree

project manager The nominated person with the responsibility and authority to deliver the project on time, within budget and within the agreed scope. Usually, but not always, the project manager is involved in the project initiation, planning, implementation and close

project (master) schedule The definitive, up-to-date list of project activities, with intended start and finish dates

project network A flow chart depicting the sequence in which a project's terminal elements are to be completed by showing terminal elements and their dependencies

project objectives Objectives define the target. They are the end of the project, the reaching of which is considered necessary for the achievement of planned benefits. No project should start without clear and understood objectives

project plan A list of activities that are necessary to complete a project on time and within budget. These activities are often grouped into phases and will sometimes show ownership, timing and dependencies. Plans can also be displayed in a graphical format

project planning The process of creating and maintaining a plan against which the delivery of the project will be implemented

project portfolio A group of projects. If they are related or have a common shared goal, they would be referred to as a programme

project review board (PRB) The body of senior executives whose strategic role is to review the progress of current projects and authorise contingency funding where necessary. This should also be the formal commissioning body by which new projects are authorised and approved. Project managers often formally report to the PRB

project review meeting (PRM) A meeting at which progress against plan is reviewed, as a minimum. In practice, project issues, risks and decisions are also addressed. There is a trend to schedule PRMs against milestones

project risk A potential problem associated with the delivery of the project and its objectives. Each risk should be identified and quantified in terms of probability and impact, before agreeing and planning what actions will be taken and by whom

project specialist A team member brought in for a specific technical or content reason. Usually only involved for a short duration, the specialist delivers against agreed objectives and is then released (to other projects). The use of project specialists should be planned in advance as they are a costly and rare resource

project sponsor Sometimes called 'executive sponsor', this is usually a member of the senior management team with responsibility for championing the project. The project sponsor will set the overall objectives for the project, select the project manager and ensure sufficient resources and budget throughout

project team The group of people responsible for completion of project activities in order for the project to achieve its goal

project template A formatted document designed to aid project managers in all phases of project management and especially in project reporting. Each company's methodology should use templates

reports Monitoring of performance is crucial for the effective management of projects. Reports are either on a time basis (e.g. monthly) or on an event basis (e.g. completion of stage 1). Too many reports slow a project; too few precede a loss of control

resources matrix A two-dimensional grid that shows which people (or other resources such as facilities, equipment and consumables) will be required on which part of the project (or projects) and when

resource planning The process by which resources required are applied to the project plan. As a result, project plans or resource availability may change. Many tools and techniques can be used in resource planning and management

resources In project management terminology, resources are required to carry out the project tasks. They can be people, equipment, facilities, funding, or anything else capable of definition (usually other than labour) required for the completion of a project activity

responsibility assignment matrix (RAM) At its most simple, the RAM is a chart/matrix that shows who is responsible for what activities and to what level

risk management The process of mitigating the impact of identified risks. The actions taken will be preventive or contingent. In either case they need to be planned into the project plan

risk register (or risk log) A list containing information on the identified and collected project risks that have been identified. It is continually updated and assessed and should form the basis for decisions made by the project team on altering and amending activities or even deliverables

roles and responsibilities The formal process within project management by which individuals and teams know what they have to contribute towards the successful delivery of the project. The clearer the roles are made, the better the commitment

scope creep The 'moving goalposts' syndrome by which the scope of the project changes, either formally or, most likely, informally. This most often occurs when the scope of a project is not precisely defined or documented and the implementation of a project is poorly controlled

scope statement Often included in a project charter, the scope statement usually details the project objectives and deliverables. It may sometimes also outline what is not included ('out of scope')

screening The formal procedure by which the PRB or other body assesses projects and their deliverables. As a result of screening, some projects are made priorities within a portfolio, while some may be rejected

skills matrix A simple table used to assess current skills available in a company against the needs of the project. Any 'gaps' that appear in several projects should be addressed by training, coaching, recruitment or possibly a change in project scope

SMART An acronym that helps to define objectives: specific, measurable, achievable (or agreed), realistic, time bound

stage-gate process A structured process or methodology used in project management to check progress and minimise risks throughout the project's life cycle. Each part of the project has clearly defined outputs ('stages') or deliverables and progress is checked and deliverables assessed ('gates') before further progress is permitted

stakeholders Individuals or groups affected by the project and its outcome. This could include both those who are positively and negatively affected. Stakeholder management (or stakeholder analysis) is about managing expectations and communicating with these individuals and groups

sub-projects A technique by which a project can be broken down into constituent parts based upon certain criteria. These 'chunks' can be called sub-projects. For instance, a project could be broken down by geography, by which all tasks in one country are grouped in a sub-project and managed by a sub-project manager or specialist

task time The hours of effort or input involved in completing a deliverable. Often used for costing and budgeting purposes within projects, it should not be confused with duration, which is most often used for scheduling and planning

task types There are three types of task: fixed duration (the task will take a fixed time to complete, no matter how many resources are allocated); resource driven (the time taken to complete the task is a function of the resources allocated); and resource limited (the duration of a task will reduce to a certain point when resources are allocated, but after a certain point it will reduce no further)

terminal element The lowest level of activity within a WBS. This is sometimes simply called 'task' or 'work package'. It cannot be logically subdivided any further

terms of reference (ToR) A document that describes the purpose and structure of a project. It often defines the vision, objectives, scope and deliverables, stakeholders, roles and responsibilities, resources, financials and quality plans, WBS and schedule. The terms of reference set out a road map for the project

work The amount of effort applied (input) to produce a deliverable or to accomplish a task

work breakdown structure (WBS) A list of activities and sub-activities that need to be accomplished to deliver the value of the project. The WBS should include 100 per cent of the activities defined by the scope of the project

INDEX

Items in **bold** relate to entries in the Glossary.

FAST TRACK TO SUCCESS

9780273719908

9780273721789

9780273721802

9780273719885

9780273719922

9780273721765

EVERYTHING YOU NEED TO ACCELERATE YOUR CAREER